HAUNTED
DAKOTAS

HAUNTED DAKOTAS

GHOSTS AND STRANGE PHENOMENA OF THE PEACE GARDEN AND MOUNT RUSHMORE STATES

ANDY WEEKS

Globe
Pequot

ESSEX, CONNECTICUT

Globe Pequot

An imprint of Globe Pequot, the trade division of
The Rowman & Littlefield Publishing Group, Inc.
4501 Forbes Blvd., Ste. 200
Lanham, MD 20706
www.rowman.com

Distributed by NATIONAL BOOK NETWORK

British Library Cataloguing in Publication Information available

Library of Congress Cataloging-in-Publication Data
Names: Weeks, Andy, author.
Title: Haunted Dakotas : ghosts and strange phenomena of the Peace Garden and Mount Rushmore states / Andy Weeks.
Description: Lanham : Globe Pequot, [2023] | Series: Haunted | Includes bibliographical references.
Identifiers: LCCN 2022059449 (print) | LCCN 2022059450 (ebook) | ISBN 9781493069811 (paperback) | ISBN 9781493069828 (ebook)
Subjects: LCSH: Haunted places—Dakota Territory. | Ghosts—Dakota Territory.
Classification: LCC BF1472.U6 W43554 2023 (print) | LCC BF1472.U6 (ebook) | DDC 133.109783—dc23/eng/20230322
LC record available at https://lccn.loc.gov/2022059449
LC ebook record available at https://lccn.loc.gov/2022059450

♾️™ The paper used in this publication meets the minimum requirements of American National Standard for Information Sciences—Permanence of Paper for Printed Library Materials, ANSI/NISO Z39.48-1992.

In memory of my mother-in-law, Linda.
Thank you for being a great second mom,
for always supporting my writing projects,
and for impacting my life.
I miss you!

CONTENTS

INTRODUCTION

So many ghosts, and forms of fright,
Have started from their graves to-night,
They have driven sleep from mine eyes away;
I will go down to the chapel and pray.
—*Henry Wadsworth Longfellow*

Ghosts are real.

At least that's what about half of Americans say in separate nationwide surveys conducted in recent years by Gallup and the Pew Research Center. Findings from the surveys indicate that belief in the paranormal is on the rise. Does this mean more people are having encounters with the ghostly and strange? Perhaps.

Likewise, the subject of ghosts remains popular in mass media; one can find everything from regional books, such as this one, to thicker tomes and novels with ghostly antagonists. And there is a hearty supply of television shows depicting paranormal investigators on the prowl for evidence of life beyond the grave and blockbuster movies, such as the recent *The Conjuring* series, with their haunted houses and otherworldly themes.

Belief in strange phenomena is not tied to the subject of ghosts only. In a different survey conducted in July 2021, it was found that four in ten people claim to have seen what they believe to be something from out of this world. "While Americans are still inclined to think UFOs are *not* alien spacecraft, close to half believe alien life forms exist *beyond Earth*," according to the 2021 Gallup report. In that article it referred to a poll taken two years earlier, noting, "A June 2019 poll found 49% of Americans believing there are 'people somewhat like ourselves' living on other planets. A much larger percentage, 75%, said that 'life of some form' exists elsewhere in the universe."

Do some of these strange craft seen in our night skies carry life forms that travel millions of miles to enact encounters with us earthlings? According to the statistics, some people really do believe that.

Also, in the "strange phenomena" or unexplained category are weird creature sightings that baffle our known understanding of our galaxy's third planet and what life forms call it home. For example, "Nessie," the Loch Ness Monster, or Harry the Sasquatch, otherwise known as Bigfoot, both which have a long and many-varied sightings-by-people history. As for the latter, alleged sightings of the uncouth Sasquatch have been reported from the Pacific Northwest to the Appalachian Mountains—including right here in the Dakotas. The Peace Garden State also is home to at least one lake monster legend.

In the world in which we live, there also are tales about real-life vampires, werewolves, and witches. The paramount question that arises with each of these topics is this: Are the stories true?

HISTORY, LORE, AND HAUNTINGS

Something we should keep in mind whenever we study the paranormal and other strange phenomena is that many of the tall tales we come across, legend and folklore, usually have some basis in fact. Barring the stories shared by first-hand witnesses, old stories often get embellished or exaggerated over time. It is something akin to telling the first person standing in a long line of storytellers that grandma's silver wig was lost in the wind and grandpa went running off to fetch it for her. Once the story reaches the end of the line, it isn't quite the same as it was when it started. Having been passed from one ear to another, now the story is about grandpa who got lost in a storm when he went looking for his gray toupee.

Another way to view this is to understand that folklore is an exaggeration of something that really did happen. We can turn to Hollywood and the aforementioned *The Conjuring* series for some clarification. *The Conjuring* and its sequels are based on the real-life case files of Ed and Lorraine Warren, a husband-and-wife paranormal investigating team who rose to fame in the 1970s after their investigation of the Amityville Horror House in Long Island, New York. *The Conjuring 2* (2016), based on the true-life Amityville crime, depicts hauntings the couple supposedly explored at the infamous house, as well as paranormal phenomenon at another haunted house in Enfield, England. Hollywood, however, throughout the franchise, exaggerates the Warrens' case files with over-the-top and unbelievable episodes of ghostly activity—such as a doll that writes crayon on the walls and ceiling; a tall, morphing, crooked man that appears in physical form to haunt a susceptible victim; and a vengeful nun who wreaks havoc at a secluded convent.

These are excellent characterizations of things that scare us, making for great entertainment in a darkened theater, but, in most cases, ghosts are not so bold.

In short, the Warren case files may be real, but it is unlikely that the extreme paranormal activity explored on the big screen happened that way in real life. The movies say as much during the credits scroll. It is much the same with folklore and legend. Such stories often are based on real incidents or episodes, but they also are often exaggerated tales of such events.

This volume contains both experiences that real people have had with the paranormal and tales that fall better into the category of folklore and legend, having been passed down through a number of years and, as such, have perhaps become exaggerated along the way. It is the experiences and perspectives of real people that I enjoy and appreciate most. I also enjoy the background, the history behind the hauntings. It is a commonly held belief that there can be no haunting without a history. I have tried to share some history of the sites depicted in these stories, while being mindful to not neglect the weightier matter of why you most likely picked this book up in the first place: for the ghost stories.

As I said earlier, Hollywood's depiction of a haunting is usually not how it played itself out in real life. But that's not to say that paranormal activity cannot be extreme. Indeed, it can be, and in the following pages you'll read about a few individuals who have had close encounters—and very frightening episodes—with entities beyond our natural world. In some cases, the paranormal *is* in-your-face bold.

Among the more frightening episodes are of ghosts and other unseen entities physically attacking individuals, appearing as full-bodied apparitions, moving objects and damaging property. Within these pages, you'll read about a team of North Dakota paranormal investigators who have had many flagrant experiences with unseen entities, a saloon owner who witnessed an apparition in his business, and a South Dakota woman who claims she and her family have been terrorized by at least one unfriendly spirit. You'll also meet one of the world's youngest demonologists, who saw his first apparition at age twelve and many more since then, and a savvy YouTuber for whom the paranormal is anything but *not* normal. It has followed him his whole life and he has come to accept that it is part of his own existence to have such experiences. Before we get to these haunts and others, however, there are a few more things we need to review.

TYPES OF HAUNTINGS

For those who believe in the paranormal, there exist at least six different classifications of hauntings (some people may claim there are more).

Residual: A residual haunting is the most common type of paranormal occurrence. But what exactly is a residual haunting? There might not be an "exact" definition for this or any other type of haunting, but here's one way to look at it: when something tragic happens at a location, the negative energy from the occurrence is "blasted" into the space-time continuum where it then can repeatedly replay itself, much like a broken record does on a turntable. However, I tend to believe that residual hauntings are the past's imprint not only of something tragic that has happened but also of life's other instances. We all are creatures of habit; we all experience many aspects of what it means to be a mortal every day—health and sickness, happiness and sadness, laughter and tears. We all are caught up in our own daily routines. Life is an emotional journey. Why can't the experiences we have daily, especially as they repeat themselves in our own routines, make a lasting impact in that same time-space continuum? The phantom footsteps on the stairs or the creaking of a door you may hear, for instance, may not be anything "new," per se, but a recording from the past.

Intelligent: An intelligent haunting is what most ghost seekers want to tap into when they go on a paranormal investigation. They may ask the alleged spirit questions, sometimes even asking it to perform an activity such as knocking on a wall, closing a door, or turning on a light in an effort to provoke a response. Because an intelligent haunting is not a blast from the past but a manifestation of an actual entity, it will respond in real time, such as performing the requested knock on the wall. In this and other ways of interaction, an intelligent haunting will try to communicate with the living.

Poltergeist: A poltergeist, translated to English, means "noisy ghost," likes to play tricks on, or in other ways unnerve, its human victims. It most often does this by moving inanimate objects, throwing items, making lights turn off and on, or doors open and close, et cetera. These hauntings are different than intelligent hauntings because they are not necessarily trying to communicate with their mortal victims but, rather, to scare or play jokes on them. It's believed that poltergeists often are manifested around teenage girls. These might be prankster ghosts, but that doesn't mean they're friendly. Obviously, an entity that seeks to frighten and scare is not in the same league as our decades-old favorite TV ghost, Casper.

Demons: The most sinister and frightening of all hauntings are those caused by demons, unembodied (not disembodied) entities who seek to torment and scare their victims. These entities come from the very bands of hell and, if allowed, will seek the possession of their victims. Demons are real and are mentioned throughout history, including in holy writ. They cause anxiety, depression, and fear, and they seek the misery and control of their victims. Those who believe in God know, however, that the Father of creation is mightier than these anxious entities from hell.

Shadow People: Often in paranormal circles there is talk of shadow people, or shadow figures. Some individuals say they have seen these dark entities most often from their peripheral vision, moving about; others claim to have seen them in a darkened room or even outside. Sometimes shadow figures have been known to appear at one's bedside, or in other locations. One person I interviewed for a previous book said he saw shadow figures in his driveway, as if they were playing hide-and-seek near his parked vehicle. While there is much we do not know about shadow people, their purpose remaining largely unknown, their intent seems to be acknowledged: to frighten and make afraid.

Doppelganger: The least common of all paranormal occurrences is the doppelganger, which in the English vernacular means "double walker, known as a person's 'evil twin.'" Such hauntings have been documented, but they are rare and hardly ever reported, according to paranormal experts. Still, these are frightening visages not to be trifled with. If you pass yourself on the sidewalk, it is best to keep going in the opposite direction.

A TRAVELOG THROUGH THE DAKOTAS

Ghost stories may send a few chills up your back, but history should warm you up. And the Dakotas, while being some of the last states admitted to the Union, are full of long and fascinating histories. Much of their history—and much that makes it fascinating—are the Indigenous tribes whose influence, thankfully, is still felt in the region today. The white man may have raped the land long ago, but no matter how they may have tried, they did not diminish the heritage and culture that was here long before the settlers arrived.

This book, which covers topics and tales from both the Dakotas, is divided primarily into two sections—North Dakota and South Dakota—each with subsections of different regions.

As you can tell by its size, this book is not a comprehensive volume about the history or the hauntings of the Dakotas. A few other books, listed in the "Further Reading" appendix, help to tell the larger story. But I hope this book is a worthy addition to the growing library about the haunts in these two sometimes overlooked states. I hope it serves as a pleasant way for you to pass a few hours.

It is my wish that the tales told here spark curiosity and interest for further study of Dakota history, including the stranger sides of these unique states. Lastly, I hope what is told here about ghosts and other strange phenomena in the prairieland will create at least a few goose pimples for you. Keep the lights on!

NORTH DAKOTA is an unassuming state, but it is rich in history. It also has its share of the unexplained, making it a fun place to learn about and explore. There is plenty that goes bump in the night in the Peace Garden State.

Armchair visitors may have an artificial knowledge of this mystic place. They may think, for instance, especially with all the images of winter found on the internet, that North Dakota is nothing but a year-round frozen tundra. But that's not the case. It is, indeed, bitingly frigid in the winter but also has pleasant summers, plentiful sunflower fields, and wildlife that add beauty and character to the state. It is home to rolling hills and flatlands, endless scenes of wind-whipped prairie grass and robust agriculture fields, and both urban areas and rural communities. It is a nice place to visit and a good place to live and work.

North Dakota, which gained statehood on November 2, 1889, and encompasses some 70,698 square miles, is the fourth least populated state in the Union. With a population of 762,062, by 2019 census estimates, it trails only Alaska (724,357), Vermont (623,251), and Wyoming (581,075). As such, North Dakota affords opportunities not available in more heavily congested areas. It just doesn't feel crowded. Even in the larger cities, such as Grand Forks or Fargo, the latter being the state's largest, there is still the hometown vibe. The people in this expansive state are, for the most part, welcoming and friendly.

Its rugged climate may be why North Dakota is an often-overlooked state; but it is, quite frankly, one of the country's hidden gems and people are surprised when they come here to find it offers much more than white winters. It also has an interesting history.

Long before North Dakota became a state, it was part of the French-controlled land known as La Louisiane, or the Louisiana Territory. It came into possession by the United States when President Thomas Jefferson obtained the territory in 1803 as part of the Louisiana Purchase. The area later to be called North Dakota and South Dakota then became part of the Minnesota and Nebraska territories and, finally in 1861, the Dakota Territory. By this time, statehood was only twenty-seven years away—mere seconds in the biological clock of a nation's history.

North Dakota saw a significant population boom between 1879 and 1886, when more than 100,000 people entered the territory. A second wave of migrants, many of them of Scandinavian and Germanic origin, arrived beginning in about 1905, and by 1920 the young state had 646,872 residents. Norwegian culture makes up an interesting and colorful part of North Dakota history, and many sites around the state tell of these industrious people.

Some of those historic footprints are the ghosts and lore that remain. As with any history, there are the occasional blight spots; wherever there is sunshine, there usually is shadow, and North Dakota has its share of gloom. Here, among its many layers of history and topography, are some strange tales to be told, adding to the interesting tale that is North Dakota. There are reports of strange-creature sightings, such as Bigfoot and lake monsters, and reports of UFOs and other unexplained phenomena that appear in the night sky. But mostly there are tales of the ghostly. And if the stories hold true, some of the ghosts are quite obtrusive.

THE WESTERN EDGE

THE FOUNDER OF MEDORA, A LINGERING SPIRIT, AND AN OLD CHATEAU

THE CHATEAU DE MORES, MEDORA

There's a little of France in North Dakota—particularly, the stately Chateau de Mores, a spacious two-story building constructed in 1883 near present-day Medora. The property, part of the Chateau de Mores State Historic Site, is a time capsule of life on the rolling prairie more than one hundred years ago.

Medora and the surrounding area have a lot of interesting history; some of it is tied to two charismatic figures: the founder of Medora and builder of the chateau, the Marquis de Morès, and a man by the name of Theodore Roosevelt. Interestingly, both men crossed paths, and both impacted—and were impacted by—the Badlands. Roosevelt, for instance, said his time spent ranching in Dakota Territory was a sort of spiritual journey for him, giving him fodder for the successes he would later achieve and the presidency he one day would assume. His legacy is forever entwined with North Dakota by the national park that carries his name.

The Marquis also left his mark, including the chateau—meaning a large French-style country house—that he built for his family in 1883. The twenty-six-room chateau is located not quite a mile west and south of Medora and overlooks the town where other historic markers lie: Chimney Park and De Mores Memorial Park, both which have ties to the Marquis, a French aristocrat and entrepreneur who imprinted his legacy with these and other now-historic landmarks.

Born to the Duke of Vallombrosa in 1858, Antoine-Amédée-Marie-Vincent Manca Amat de Vallombrosa more readily went by the honorary title of the Marquis de Morès et de Montemaggiore, or the Marquis de Morès. Titles aside, he received much of his wealth from his in-laws, and when he came to this neck of Dakota Territory, he named the emerging town after his wife, Medora Marie von Hoffman, daughter of a wealthy Wall Street banker.

He built the chateau as a seasonal residence and hunting lodge and had it ready for when his wife joined him in 1884. It is a long building adorned with several windows, as if many eyes are keeping watch among the prairie. Here the couple and their daughter, along with a number of servants, occupied the chateau only seasonally for three years, but, during that time, Lady de Morès adorned it with some of the fine furnishings of the day. It is believed that she had what some may call a "tomboy" side of her personality. She was a good shot, did well on a horse, and likely joined her husband on some of his hunting adventures.

While he waited for the Lady de Morès to arrive, the Marquis kept his entrepreneurial spirit alive. Before western Dakota boomed with oil, the cattle industry was all the rage. Seeing more dollar signs in his future, he opened a slaughterhouse and meatpacking plant in 1883, the same year he built the chateau, with the idea to send beef by refrigerated railcar to the more lucrative restaurants and businesses of the eastern states. His theory was that having cattle slaughtered straight off the range, instead of being shipped live to the Chicago stockyards, would be more lucrative because slaughtered beef would retain its heft and not lose weight as live animals would during transit.

His business didn't have the lasting effect he had hoped for, and his fortuitous plans were short-lived when, in 1886, the operation shut down. When the family left the Dakota Badlands for their native Europe, the markers they established remained, a little French influence in North Dakota. The chateau, specifically, is a venue to the past in another way, for it is rumored that some of the old-time spirits have remained. Most notably, one of them may be the spirit of Medora herself.

Legend has it that the apparition of a female spirit has been seen at the chateau, and not only at one location but apparently in many places around the property. According to some stories, ghostly caretakers have also been seen on the property, going about their work as they did when they were alive, seemingly not knowing that they now go through their routines as disembodied spirits instead of donned with flesh-and-blood.

Other paranormal activity at the chateau are lights that have been reported to turn on in the house when no one is in the building, cold spots that have been detected at some locations at various times of day, and ghostly laughter heard inside the house when it is obvious no human could be blamed.

Are these residual hauntings of people from the past, playing or repeating what had been done here while the Marquis and his family remained? Or are these spirits of the more intelligent kind, making their presence known from time to time because of their attachment to the historic property? Perhaps they are making sure the Marquis's chateau is cared for and safely protected. But if so, what about the alleged darker entities that are said to also have a presence here?

More frightening than the phantom sounds and a female apparition are the dark shadows that have been known to creep at certain places on the property, sending chills up the spines of their weary witnesses.

Shadow figures, according to paranormal circles, do not emit positive vibes. Different theories exist about what shadow figures may be. Some say they are another manifestation of a ghost, though the more common belief is that they are different from ghosts in that they are deemed nonhuman entities, dark masses whose sole ambition is to cause anxiety and fear. They can be shapeless, but often they take the shape of a real person—thus their name, shadow people. Ironically, for those who report seeing a shadow person that lacks a discernable outline, it is common to describe the entity as wearing a hat, such as a fedora. These entities of black mass are quick, often with odd movements.

There is much we don't know about shadow people. Easier to explain is why the spirit of Lady Morès may have remained. There obviously are some attachments for her, such as the nearby town named after her and the chateau she devoted much time and attention to during her and her family's stay. What drew her spirit back—the town, the chateau, or both?

She visited for the last time—at least as a mortal—after her husband died.

Despite any creepiness that some people allege happens here, the chateau retains its interesting spot in Dakota history and is surely worth a visit. Come here to experience the past in Dakota Territory.

According to the State Historical Society of North Dakota, which manages the property, the chateau, now a "historic house museum . . . contains many of the original furnishings and personal effects of the de Morès family." Tours of the house, as described on the Historical Society website, take about an hour and are available during the summer months for the price of admission.

The Historical Society also offers a "History Alive!" program: "History Alive! programs explore the lives and times of local residents from decades gone by, combining theater arts with history. The 20-minute monologues are based on original letters, diaries, and other documents, many from the archives of the State Historical Society of North Dakota." The free program, at the time of this writing, is presented on weekends with times listed both in morning and afternoon on Saturdays and Sundays from June through August.

Other related sites in the area include the De Morès Memorial Park, located in downtown Medora, which has a bronze statue of the Marquis that was donated by his sons in 1926.

Chimney Park, or the site of the Marquis's old slaughterhouse and the old railroad spur, sits on the western edge of Medora. The Historical Society says the building burned in 1907 but the facility's tall brick chimney was left standing. In case the reminiscence of beef causes a stir in your stomach, a picnic area is located next to the plant. Bring your lunch!

A MEAN-TEMPERED GHOST CALLED THE ENFORCER

BILLINGS COUNTY COURTHOUSE MUSEUM, MEDORA

Ghosts are many—and extremely active—at the Billings County Courthouse Museum, located at 475 4th Street in Medora. Site manager Bambi Mansfield, who had been with the museum for eight years by the time we visited on August 16, 2022, said she has experienced paranormal activity inside the building for all of those years. Sometimes the activity has been subtle, other times more blunt. In the week leading up to our conversation, she said activity at the building had ramped up. Books—thick, heavy tomes—flew off counters; chains on display that stretched from one wall to another started bouncing; and an unnerving presence was felt in parts of the building.

Mansfield, who said she's experienced the supernatural ever since her cardiac arrest at age sixteen, said she is not frightened by the paranormal—but that there is one unnerving presence she doesn't like. She and her staff have dubbed him "the Enforcer."

While there is likely nothing malevolent in the building, according to Wendy Kimble and Stephanie Pinkey, co-founders of Paranormal Investigators of North Dakota based in Minot, the entity called the Enforcer, whose spirit could have belonged to a jail guard during the courthouse's prime, is quite ornery—maybe even mean or ill-tempered. Mansfield said there is a particular room in the building where the atmosphere changes. His presence isn't always felt there, but when it is, you don't want to go inside. There is just a bad vibe about it, she said.

Managed by the Billings County Historical Society, the Billings County Courthouse Museum was built in the 1880s. A remodel project took place in 1913 and the building served the county as a courthouse for a number of years. It was added to the National Register of Historic Places in 1977 and took on new life in 1986 when it became a museum.

Its exhibits are not what one would usually expect at a museum: frontier farm and ranch memorabilia. Here, exhibits depict automotive items, barbed wire and fencing material, farming implements, military memorabilia, and other displays—exhibits that give a nod to the rustic, western-style history that is Medora.

The aforementioned mysteriously bouncing chains on display in one of the exhibits stretch from wall to wall; they don't touch the ground. And yet those who saw them move—there were more eyes on them than only Mansfield's—were left dumbfounded by what they had witnessed. How could they move like that when pulled across the room and fastened to the walls? What entity could do that and, perhaps more importantly, why? Was it a poltergeist? Was it the Enforcer? And, if so, what was its message? Or was it intended to only frighten?

Mansfield, who considers herself an empath—someone with the ability to understand the emotional state of another—doesn't know. When it comes to the paranormal, some things are left unexplained. However, some of the spirits at the old building seem to be lost, and she has tried to help some of them to move on. She's had some success, including helping a little boy's spirit who, while a mortal, died in a fire. His shoes were found decades later and, through research, she found out who the little boy likely was. She brought the shoes, which had been stored at the facility, to his gravesite, and his presence, which had previously been felt in the museum, has not been detected since.

A BAR AND ITS GHOSTLY PATRONS

LITTLE MISSOURI SALOON, MEDORA

Not long after Jim Bridger bought the Little Missouri Saloon in Medora in 2012, he witnessed something that, to this day, cannot be explained except in the context of the paranormal. While cooking in the facility's kitchen after hours not long after he purchased the property, he saw a man in a baseball cap walk up the stairs to the second floor to, Bridger assumed, use the restroom. Normally, Bridger wouldn't have given it a second thought, but on this night, it gave him plenty to think about. He explained:

I was cooking at the time. The kitchen hadn't been remodeled yet so there was a full view of the staircase and dining room area up until the figure turned the corner to the bathrooms. The kitchen is in the opposite corner of the staircase so the view was good.

I was in the kitchen cleaning and cooking a couple last meals to go downstairs to the saloon. The upstairs dining was closed already but the saloon level remained open. There were swinging saloon doors at the bottom of the staircase, which are always closed when (the) top level closes, and they are loud so it was always easy to hear when somebody came upstairs due to the old doors making noise. This time there was no noise and that's why I found it a little odd to see such a person walking in [the] bathroom corridor.

What was odder still, the man he saw trek up the stairs never came back down. After a few minutes, Bridger went up those same steps to check on the man.

No one was there.

Hmm, Bridger thought—and goose pimples danced up his back. "It made every hair on my neck stand up," he said. "That was freaky. I am a skeptic. I'm skeptical of things like this, but that was weird. That was strange."

Bridger had just had his first encounter with the paranormal. As a saloon owner, he knows all about the spirits that imbibe, but the kind that haunt was new territory for him—something he didn't expect when he purchased the property, named after the Little Missouri River that flows through the area. Though the establishment has changed ownership over the years, its name has remained the same and the saloon continues to be a popular stop for visitors and locals alike. And according to the stories that Bridger continues to hear from staff and customers, some of its patrons from yesteryear have never left.

We see tens of thousands of customers every year just in the summertime, and people will walk up to me and say, "Did you feel that?" Or "Is this place haunted? Because I've been feeling something looking over my shoulder the whole time." Or "It felt like something touched me, but I've been sitting at a table alone." I started hearing stories like that, and different organizations that search for paranormal activities have been coming out and using some equipment, listening to stories from cooks about pots and pans falling off the wall or of mysterious noises of people walking upstairs when there is nobody there.

Though he has gotten a little more used to the strange happenings of his restaurant since his encounter with the apparition that wore a baseball cap, he still doesn't quite know how to classify the experiences that seem common fodder for visitors. To help, he invited a paranormal investigating team to see what they could come up with.

Enter Wendy Kimble and Stephanie Pinkey, co-founders of Paranormal Investigators of North Dakota. Based in Minot, in the central region of the state, the women and their group travel the state to investigate claims of paranormal activity. The team, using technical equipment to detect thermal activity and other gadgets to prompt and record phantom sounds or movement, have both debunked and verified a number of alleged hauntings across the Peace Garden State. But sometimes they haven't needed any tool but their own senses to have interactions with the unseen spirits that linger.

The Little Missouri Saloon, located at 440 3rd Street in Medora, is a place where they have done both—obtained evidence of paranormal activity by using equipment and had up-close and personal encounters with unseen entities. While there might be a darker presence in the facility's basement, the activity at the Little Missouri is not malicious. A little flirtatious maybe, yes—perhaps even obnoxious—but malevolent, not likely.

Among the experiences they had during their initial investigation of the property in early 2022, Kimble and Pinkey both confirmed what had been reported by others—the feeling of having been touched by unseen hands, sometimes in inappropriate ways. "We didn't see anything physical, but Stephanie and I both were touched," Kimble said in a virtual meeting on May 16, 2022, noting the first sensation she felt was as if someone was touching her toes. The sensation then moved to her leg. "First it was my left leg, my knee, a little bit of my inner thigh. It moved to my shoulder and then it slowly moved over to Stephanie, where it played with her hair, [putting what felt] like fingers down her back. The spirits are definitely a little flirtatious."

Perhaps more than flirtatious—inappropriate, even for a ghost.

Another investigating member who was there that night received a different kind of spectral touch. She felt as if she had been punched in the arm. "She had a big red mark on her arm, and the next morning I took pictures of it because it was still a little red," Pinkey said.

At one point, Pinkey felt as if someone had grabbed her arm harshly as well, so much so that the imprints of fingers were left behind. As the two discussed the situation during our virtual meeting, Kimble came up with one conclusion for these physical manifestations: "If you [and the other investigator] were both talking to Jim, it could have been a female spirit that felt connected to him, maybe a bit possessive, like 'why are you talking to my man?' You could see three fingerprints on Stephanie's arm, like somebody had grabbed her, like they were trying to say, 'Hey, back off.' Stephanie was talking to Jim when she was grabbed."

"Yep, I was," Pinkey said. "It wasn't super aggressive. I think, like Wendy said, the spirit just didn't want me talking to Jim. Or maybe it was because when one of the other entities were touching us, she was getting jealous. I don't know."

Ghosts or not, the food and beverage industry is not an easy business to be in. It was even tougher during the early stages of a global pandemic that started in 2020. But Bridger has made a fine go of it since taking over the establishment— and navigating the pandemic—and the saloon remains a favorite watering hole for many: local people, out-of-towners, and, apparently, even the ghosts.

THE FORGOTTEN HOSPITAL

SENTINEL BUTTE

Jim Bridger may have had his first wake-up call to the reality of the paranormal while cooking in his saloon one night not many months after he purchased the property, but it wouldn't be his last. The second instance that caused his neck hair to stand on end happened at another property he purchased, this one an old house that, in its earliest days, once held the medically sick and infirm.

Bridger bought the property in 2013, a year after he purchased the Little Missouri Saloon, and said he originally planned to tear it down and build employee housing for those working in the oil industry. "But then an oil boom ended the immediate need for housing, so I just let it remain there," he said, noting he is unsure when the structure was built but that he believes it underwent a remodel sometime in the 1950s.

"After that it became a boarding house for teachers," he explained, noting a family once also lived in the house "and put antiquated plumbing into it. Prior to that there was no water, just an outhouse which still stands. They moved out and it has been empty for decades."

Except for the ghosts.

The former occupants—patients and otherwise—of the two-story, seven-room structure have been gone a long time, but it seems that something about the place has attracted other beings to inhabit it. During an investigation in early 2022, during the same period that Wendy Kimble and Stephanie Pinkey investigated the strange goings-on at the Little Missouri Saloon, they spent an afternoon at this vacant building. It was an afternoon full of paranormal activity.

Bridger said an experience at the old building was the second time in his life that he was freaked out by something he couldn't explain. Kimble and Pinkey said they often use objects with sensors that alert to energy spikes, such as a music box or stuffed animal, to try to get a response from the supernatural world. A music box might hold interest for the spirit of a female. And if a child's spirit is present, it might be interested in the stuffed animal. Both objects, as well as radiating electromagnetism (REM) pods and electromagnetic field (EMF) meters, were used during their investigation of the hospital. Each of them detected activity.

In theory, the REM Pod radiates its own electromagnetic field, making it easier for spirits to use the pod to communicate. The pod, which has multicolored lights atop it, can detect when something is moving in or out of this field. "The theory is that when energy or someone passes by the sensor it plays a little, creepy song," Pinkey said in reference to the music box. They said music played a number of times during their investigation in various locations in the building—on a shelf in a room, and in a closet, where, surprisingly, it went off repeatedly for several minutes straight, "without hesitation," Pinkey said, explaining that whenever the music played, their electromagnetic field detector recorded extremely high readings. "The spikes were so high that I actually could not register them with the EMF detector."

They also experimented with the REM Pod, at one time placing it on the floor next to where it is believed a patient bed once sat. It would detect movement on and off.

The most dramatic event of the day was when the group ended their investigation and was getting ready to leave. Pinkey retrieved the music box, removed the batteries, and placed it in their vehicle as they were preparing to leave for the day. Once back at the doorstep, as Bridger was locking up, he said: "Hey, do you hear that? Is the music box still inside?"

"No," Pinkey said. "It's in the car. I just put it away. There are no batteries in it." She stopped to listen and said of the experience, "Oh my goodness! I could hear the music box going off inside!"

The hair on Bridger's neck stood on end.

Physically, the item was packed inside the vehicle with the other equipment, but something had recorded or imitated the sound from inside—a residual haunting of an occurrence that had happened only moments before.

That may have been the tip of the iceberg of the activity they witnessed that afternoon, but the sublayers to the berg were being built all that day. During their time at the building, the group heard footsteps upstairs when no living body was up there, perhaps echoing what happened in the past when doctors and nurses walked from room to room to check on patients. The investigators would go up to check things out, reset the equipment, and go back downstairs, only to again hear the same sounds of footsteps a few minutes later.

In any case, the women believe the haunting at the hospital is at least mostly residual in nature. But what about sensors going off and interactions with the music box? Isn't that activity more in line with an intelligent haunting? Not necessarily, they said. They explained that residual hauntings can also lend themselves to spiking EMF recordings. "It doesn't matter what kind of haunting it is, if it's intelligent or residual, the energy that keeps being repeated is still there," Kimble said. "It's like being stamped into quantum physics—the space-time of that area."

However, she noted that she believes there might be a bit of both—residual and intelligent hauntings at the building. "I think it was a little bit of everything," she said. "I didn't really pick up anything negative. It was crazy because each room had a different feeling, an ambiance to it, almost like one room was more anxious, one room you would feel sad, another room you wouldn't, you would feel okay. It really depends on who was there, what kind of impact they had, what happened to them."

Sentinel Butte, a dot on the map that lies on the outskirts of Medora that is small enough that if you blinked while passing through you might miss it, was founded in 1902 along the transcontinental rail line of the Northern Pacific Railway. The name comes from the prominent butte about three miles to the south, named in honor of two Arikara sentinels killed in the vicinity in 1864 by the Sioux.

The town had a short-lived history when it boomed and busted more than a century ago, at one time boasting a number of businesses and a population of nearly one thousand during its heyday between 1906 and 1910. The former hospital sits near the aforesaid rail line, which could be a cause for the paranormal activity of the facility.

The energy from the locomotives could very well be supplying some energy to the hauntings, Kimble said, making them spike in the old hospital. "One of the big things as to why this energy can keep doing what it's doing is because the railroad goes right by there. That's a constant source of energy," she explained.

Bridger has maintained the structure and many of the items inside of it, which may contribute to the hauntings. Spirits, according to paranormal circles, often attach themselves to objects they were familiar with when they were cloaked with mortality.

And Bridger, in a follow-up email, said of the building:

> *I plan on just leaving the hospital as is. I've had many offers for people to go in and strip the antique wood, doors, etc., but I just can't let that happen. Each room upstairs has old religious articles, like palms, crucifix's, medals and pictures of the Virgin Mary. Not sure if they are original or if someone put them in to ward off spirits??? Either way it adds to the creepiness of the building. There is one room with the closet door kicked out and broken. But it's broken from the inside out as if something was trying to escape. . . . Very odd.*

As a reminder to the reader, the property is privately owned and anyone caught trespassing, whether to search for ghosts or for other means, is committing a crime by so doing. Respect the property and its owner. The ghosts, apparently, are not going anywhere.

APPARITIONS AND MOVING MANNEQUINS

THE OLD ARMORY, WILLISTON

Chuck Wilder knows a lot about North Dakota history, in particular, the history of Williston. As a local historian and small-business owner, and at sixty-eight years young, his smarts didn't come from the printed page only. He personally has seen much of his town's history unfold over the past several decades. He says of his town—which, according to a 2020 population estimate, has not quite thirty 30,000 people—that it may not have always been friendly to its buildings, but it does have an interesting past. And in the end, it was good to one of its most iconic buildings, the Old Armory in downtown, in no small part thanks to Wilder's dad.

At one time, North Dakota had several armories—in places such as Bismarck, Carrington, Dickinson, Fargo, Jamestown, and Mayville—but the communities to which they belonged did not preserve them. Williston's armory is different and is the only one left standing in the state, according to Wilder.

The building at 320 1st Avenue East was constructed in 1915 and, as of this writing, remains a living part of the community as an entertainment and community venue. Entertainment Inc. has been in the building since the late 1980s, putting on plays and concerts for the public to enjoy, all for the price of a ticket. In its original life, however, the building was used to house local military personnel, including Wilder's father, who, as a young man during the Depression era, joined the National Guard. The building shared features with the other armories built across the state at the time, including a castle-like turret.

"All of these armories were built in that style. They weren't all the same—I don't think any of them are the same—but they were all built like a castle," Wilder explained. "They were all built about that same time, and Williston's is the only one that's left."

As with many historic sites and old buildings, there also are strange tales associated with the Old Armory. Perhaps the most popularly circulated story is one about mannequins in the building's basement. Wearing military uniforms from different eras, they have reportedly been seen to move of their own volition. Other strange occurrences that have been reported in the building are the sounds of whispering phantom voices heard when no one else is around.

When I spoke with Wilder on May 20, 2022, he said he hadn't heard the story about the moving mannequins, but he knew of other strange tales of the building, stories about spirits that seem to make themselves known from time to time to individuals of their choosing. "I've heard stories of spirits in the Old Armory," Wilder said. One time while entertaining family from Seattle, he took them to the building and one of the visitors, who is more sensitive to the spirit world, he noted, experienced paranormal activity in the turret room.

Wilder said one claim he has heard by at least a couple of people is that his own father may be one of the spirits who visit the building occasionally. He didn't know what to say about that personally—and said he has not experienced anything strange at the building himself, including any unexpected appearances from his progenitor—but he did say the building was important to his late father, Jerry Wilder. He was one of the people who helped make sure it is still in existence today.

"It was used until about 1958, something like that," Wilder said of the armory. "Then Williston built a new armory down by the train depot and the old one was turned over to the rec council." For the next two decades or so it was used as a sports arena, where basketball and volleyball games were held. All of that started to change during the second oil boom, when a group of people wanted to build a larger recreation center.

The Raymond Family Community Center was built and the Old Armory was left in limbo, perhaps readying for a fate much like its siblings in other parts of the state. It didn't receive the attention and upkeep it deserved and started to fall into disrepair. "It was in pretty rough shape, the windows had broken, pipes had broken, and the city was planning on tearing it down," Wilder explained. "The Elks Club, which was across the street, wanted it removed. They wanted it for a parking lot. And the law offices on the south side of the building, they wanted it for a parking lot; and the bank that was across the street from it, they wanted it for parking."

Jerry Wilder, however, saw a diamond in the rough—a gem that could be restored to its former glory and, as such, serve a continued purpose in the community and remain a historical icon to a part of North Dakota's past. "My dad is the one who is credited with saving that building," Wilder said with a touch of pride in his voice. That all happened in the 1980s, but the genesis as to why had begun many years before. Jerry joined the National Guard when he was in high school, during the depths of the Depression, and later served in World War II. A dollar was a big deal back then, and that's what Jerry received—a buck for every drill. "That meant a lot to him because they lost their farm in the '30s," Wilder said. "A dollar a week was big money for my dad's family."

When the city was considering tearing down the building, Jerry stepped up, organized a veterans' group to save it, and together they held fundraisers and did what they could to preserve its legacy. Their efforts paid off and the Old Armory is still here today, alleged ghosts and all.

The effort to save the building wasn't a simple task and would prove to be another battle Jerry would fight. In fact, Wilder believes the stress of saving the building may have worsened his father's health and contributed to his passing in 1993. "My dad had a habit of taking on projects . . . and he wouldn't let go, and that's why that armory is still there and it ultimately killed him," he said.

"I'm very proud of him for it. My dad was a humble guy. He never was out there for the bells and buzzers and all that stuff," Wilder noted. He said Williston has a habit of naming buildings for people in the community, but his dad never wanted his name on the Old Armory. "But they did name a conference room in that building after him. He was a very humble guy, but he saved that building, and I'm very proud of him for it."

The Old Armory is perhaps a ghost unto itself. The building, while not flamboyant, is a historical marker in Williston and an imprint on the larger history of the country's wars and military defense. It also serves as a tribute to those who have and continue to serve their country in its national defense. It was placed on the National Register of Historic Places in 1985 for its iconic and historical architecture—one of four buildings in the city to hold that honor. (The other buildings are the old post office building, the old junior high, and the James Memorial Arts Center.)

Among the memorabilia on display in the armory are the aforementioned mannequins, some dressed in military uniform from the different wars. Wilder said his dad was also instrumental in collecting the uniforms from past wars to place them on display, apparently something that has been continued. Their models, of course, are the mannequins.

As with most alleged haunted sites, suppositions abound about the Old Armory. Truth be told, no one knows for sure who the spirits are that may linger here. Another person I spoke with about the building who has been associated with it for a number of years said she has not experienced anything otherworldly, but, like Wilder, she knows of people who have.

Visiting the Old Armory is an enjoyable experience. Those who work here are friendly and welcoming, and the performances are entertaining and worthy of their ticket price. It's a neat building to be in—and if the mannequins do move from time to time, well, that, depending on your frame of mind and interest in the paranormal, might be an added bonus.

AN ARTS CENTER AND ITS GHOSTS

JAMES MEMORIAL ARTS CENTER, WILLISTON

There's at least one entity in the James Memorial Arts Center that likes Elvis Presley songs.

Good taste, even for a ghost. It seems to especially like the song "Hound Dog."

The team at Paranormal Investigators of North Dakota caught the dancing spirit on their SLS camera—a camera with a sensory projector that detects human shapes, even if they're not mortal—during an investigation at the century-old building on July 30, 2022. The team was recording in the stage area, playing Elvis songs, when they captured the recording. On stage was a team member, moving to the music, and sight unseen, only detected by camera, was the phantom entity, also rocking away to the 1960s jam.

It was a great capture during a night that was full of activity. The great thing about Stephanie Pinkey and Wendy Kimble and their PIND team is that they try very hard to debunk alleged paranormal activity. And during this investigation they did just that, trying to figure out the logical explanations of why loud knocking was heard on the doors—were real people outside the building pranking them? Stephanie wondered—and why their music box with infrared sensors would go off repeatedly whenever they used their walkie-talkies—was it a technical malfunction or something paranormal?

Not everything has an answer—leaving the door wider open to the mysteries of the unexplained. Like the child's spirit that was also detected in the building when, Wendy said, they had no explanation as to why a child might be there. It was an active night nonetheless, and Stephanie said equipment started going off right away.

Whatever may lurk here, Deana Novak calls the spirits at the James Memorial Arts Center her friends. As that word—friend—implies, there is nothing malicious about the entities that roam here. They are benign spirits, though perhaps—at least some of them—like to pull pranks.

Novak, who serves as president, joined the museum's board in 2009, where she served for three years before being elected president, a position she held for six years. When she stepped down, she took the role of vice president; but in 2022, the then-president resigned and Novak found herself back in the president's role.

"I'm also the primary person who hangs the art exhibits," she said. "I do that at the end of every month. I lock myself in the building with my music turned up and hang all of the art exhibits. That's when I have had experiences with the unexplained." There have been so many strange occurrences experienced by Novak and her team that she says, "We just call them our friends."

Perhaps at least some of the friends have a long history at the building.

The James Memorial was built in 1911 and was first used as a library. Basically, Novak explained, a group of ladies from the Book and Thimble Club of Williston wanted their community to have a library, and so they started fundraising with ice cream socials at the nearby train depot. Later realizing those efforts might take a while to fund their plans, they came up with the idea of asking a wealthy benefactor—in this case, Arthur Curtiss James—to help fund the ambition. "He was willing to put the money up for the building along with the money that the ladies had raised," Novak said.

The site chosen was an excavated brickyard with a hole in it. They petitioned the town to collect glass bottles and tin cans to fill the hole, and once it was filled, the building was constructed over it—not the best idea in the world. "Now a hundred and some odd years later, we're starting to understand how that's a bad idea, because our building shifts and settles as the trash beneath us degrades," Novak said. That's where the Preservation Society comes in, making sure the building, which is listed on the National Register of Historical Places, is cared for properly. The building is named after Willis James, from whom Williston receives its name. "We have a big, beautiful oil portrait of him in the vestibule when you come into the building, and we have a photograph of his son," she said.

The building has a main level and basement. A section of the building was added in the 1950s, noticeable by brick colors; the older portion is light-colored, whereas the newer addition is of an orange hue. The building was a library up until 1982 when the new Williston Public Library was constructed, and then the James sat empty. The city was going to tear it down in 1993, but once again concerned citizens stepped forward to save it. "They said, let us save it and turn it into an art center for the community," Novak said. "They worked very hard, did the fundraising and the necessary repairs and other things to get the building open. They're the reason we get to share art education opportunities and art exhibits. And we do wonderful events, community events." A visual arts club, a muzzleloader club, and several additional groups meet there. "It's kind of the hub for all of the different types of arts and activities in the community."

Apparently, ghosts like it as well, for here at least a few like to hang out. Novak said activity is not daily, but it does happen quite often, especially during times of renovation.

The experiences she has had are "unexplainable" to her. "Like I said, I'm the primary exhibit hanger, and for the last several years my favorite thing to do is lock myself in and hang art while I play music on a Bluetooth speaker. . . . Eventually, I started having little things happen."

And then the little things became bigger, more pronounced. One night she was in the lower level unwrapping an art exhibit, playing her music like she always does, when she saw a shadow dart across the doorway between the center stage and classroom. There's a handicap ramp that is made of plywood, which is loud when people walk on it, and she didn't hear any footsteps.

She paused the music, said hello to the empty air.

"There was no response," she said. "I went into the classroom and looked around. I went upstairs and looked around. There was nobody else in the building. I went back, turned my music back on, and started unwrapping—and I saw the shadow again," she explained. "I kept seeing it pass by the door probably ten times; it kept distracting me. I kept going and looking for people." The curtains were closed, it wasn't a car's headlights creating shadows. "Finally, I just said: 'Please stop, I'm trying to work.' And then I didn't see the shadow again."

Other unexplained phenomena in the building include the apparent ghost—possibly a child's spirit?—who liked to untie the shoelaces of a former worker. As Novak tells the story, the administrator would come into her office, shoelaces tied in double knots, and later when she moved away from her desk would find her laces untied. Novak explained, "The administrator said she didn't understand because they were never untied anywhere else; ever. They were doubled-knotted."

Another admin claimed to hear phantom footsteps and sounds as if the front door were opening when no one was there to do so. The distinct sounds of light switches clicking was also heard, but the lights remained off, and no one was there to push the buttons.

An entire chapter could be written about the strange happenings at the James Memorial building, but it is perhaps best to go see it for yourself. Even if you don't encounter any ghosts, it's a great place to visit. The center hosts art classes and a number of events throughout the year, fulfilling its role as a bright spot in the Williston community.

The spirits who linger here, including the Elvis fan, seem to concur.

"We just call them our friends," Novak said.

STRANGE LIGHTS ALONG THE RAILROAD TRACKS

NEW TOWN

There's nothing out of the ordinary about a train chugging along rail tracks with its front light turned on. What is extraordinary, however, is when the oncoming lights on a rail line are not caused by a locomotive. In the case of the railroad tracks that run through New Town, North Dakota, the light reportedly seen here on occasion belongs to something on the other side of existence. At least, that's what the stories say.

New Town, located at the "Heart of Lake Sakakawea," according to the New Town Chamber, sits on the Fort Berthold Indian Reservation in the northwestern part of the state. The chamber notes the town has a population of about 1,500 residents—though this is at odds with 2020 census estimates that indicate nearly 2,800 people live in the small community. It is about seventy-one and seventy-four miles, respectively, from Williston to the northwest and Minot to the northeast, both which boast significantly larger populations. Because of its proximity to Minot, New Town very nearly sits in the central region. If you add to New Town the city's statue of Earl Bunyan, the brother of fictional character Paul Bunyan, and the area's specters, the population ticks up a bit.

Legend has it that at least one entity—or does it comprise more than one?—makes itself manifest as mysterious red lights that float along the rail tracks and hover among the nearby trees. The lights have also been known to chase those daring enough to visit the tracks at night. Some of the other reported oddities that occur here may be summed up as natural phenomena, such as fluctuating temperatures and the feelings of being watched, both which may have rational explanations.

If one visits the site knowing of the red lights story, for instance, it's not a far-flung idea that the person might, by the power of suggestion, imagine that unseen eyes are watching from the darkness. Also, drops in temperature when outdoors is a natural occurrence. I have experienced this myself when driving my motorcycle along rural roadways. I'll be riding along with the constant breeze against me, then suddenly I enter a pocket of coolness unlike the warmer winds I had just experienced. Before long, as my motorbike and I cruise along, I ride out of the cold and into the more moderate temps that again surround me.

When I first experienced this, I thought it was perhaps something unexplainable, but I have since learned differently. It is quite normal. Bicyclists often experience this same type of temperature change. "For instance," reads an article on BostonBiker.org, "riding a bike, the temperature changes drastically along a route. In some areas, warmth radiates from the street and surroundings, almost as if it's held in abeyance by an invisible force. Elsewhere, cold blasts come unexpectedly out of nowhere. Usually, these cold blasts occur in and around open fields. No barrier can keep the thin, icy air in, so it drifts away from the openness. This cold air blows swiftly, so out of place in summertime."

But what does it mean when a locale, such as the site of the rail line in New Town, quickly changes temperature? It is not a moveable feast but, rather, stationary land. According to ghost hunters, such fluctuation in temperature could mean the presence of disembodied spirits.

Theories abound saying that a drop in temperature means a ghost is pulling energy, causing warm air to suddenly become cold. But also true is that ghost seekers often use thermal imaging devices to detect warm spots different from ambient temps. A warm spot on a sofa when no one visible is sitting there could mean the manifestation of a spirit who has taken up a spot on the couch. In short, there are no concrete answers as to why fluctuations in temperatures occur, but one belief is that it is a spirit's way of making itself known without the aid of ghost-hunting equipment.

Maybe there really is something paranormal that is going on in the vicinity of the old tracks. After all, the floating red lights are tougher to explain away.

But if these lights are orbs, then perhaps visitors don't need to fear them after all. In paranormal circles, red orbs—circles of light—mean something different than the color red normally does. In the normal world, red is often associated with anger or passion; but in the paranormal world, it is a sign of safety or strength.

I may have just disturbed the myth of the haunted tracks and their mysterious lights by making them seem not so ominous; but just because something may be paranormal doesn't mean it is something to fear. And in this instance, it very well could be that the red lights reportedly seen in this alleged haunted hotspot are not meant to cause alarm but act as a warning. Who's to say, but perhaps the lights, in their nonhuman element, are trying to alert visitors of the dangers of walking along a railroad track at night. You may see the light coming, but the train conductor might not see you until it's too late. And trains don't stop quickly. It is said that the lights disappear once the person they have been following reaches Main Street.

The last scenario is that this story is folklore more than anything else.

It is best to play it safe—don't walk the tracks at night. And knowing the stories about the strange phenomena, if they are true, why would you even want to?

CENTRAL
NORTH DAKOTA

THE STRANGE TALES OF TAGUS

TAGUS

If a building can be haunted, can an entire town? In the case of Tagus, a very small town—if it can be called that at all—perhaps. It seems to be populated by otherworldly entities that wreak all sorts of strange activity—or at least, that's the story that has circulated for a number of years.

Why Tagus, a once populated community in Mountrail County about forty minutes west of Minot, would attract such activity as glowing graves and running hellhounds—to list a few claims—can only be answered in the realm of guesswork. One explanation that tries to answer the question is the story about a community church that burned years ago and became a site for devil worshippers, whose presence and activity have drawn unseen forces from the netherworld. It is rumored that people who visit the site of the old church today will hear unearthly screams, believed to be from those very souls condemned to hell.

Stories also circulate about horses and cars that have disappeared, and unexplained lights appearing at night in some of the abandoned buildings when no living person is inside.

Tagus was founded in 1900, but its remote location and few amenities never seemed to attract a big crowd. Its population peak happened in about 1940 with 140 individuals, but thirty years later, in 1970, that number decreased to a whopping census count of fourteen. The town was disincorporated six years later when the last business shuttered its doors, and the area now is part of Egan Township.

The attraction of Tagus today is due, primarily, to its being a ghost town, where more ghosts—both figuratively and literally—than humans remain. But all of the stories about it being haunted are on the creepy side of paranormal. The entities rumored to be found here are not the friendly sort. One popular myth is that Tagus has an unseen stairway . . . to hell. Apparently, there are no stories that I could find of anyone venturing down those stairways. And why would they? But according to the legend, something has come up.

The stairway may be the conduit the hellhounds, with their glowing eyes, traverse into our realm, where they like to stalk weary passersby, chasing them like something out of a tale by Arthur Conan Doyle and his famous detective, Sherlock Holmes, as they investigate their strange case in the *Hound of the Baskervilles*.

This same conduit in Tagus is perhaps from where the wailing cries of damned souls emit.

These are definitely creepy tales about a North Dakota town that seems to have been all but forgotten. More real are the many abandoned buildings that, spirits aside, serve as their own ghosts to history's past. Tagus is a scenic little town, which in broad daylight seems reminiscent, if not a little remorseful, of its past. But if you visit here when night falls, do keep a lookout for those vicious hellhounds. In this case, their bite may very well be worse than their bark.

GHOSTLY VISITORS AT THE MUSEUM

TAUBE MUSEUM, MINOT

A little girl, not more than three years old, leaves her Mommy's side for only a moment or two. No one but the two are in the building and she doesn't go far from Mommy's office, but decides to explore a nearby hallway. Mommy is right around the corner.

But the young child's adventure is short-lived. Soon, she runs back to the office and into her Mommy's arms, crying and in fright.

"What's the matter?" Mommy asks.

The girl, in a young child's vocabulary, tells her that someone was in the hallway; someone who frightened her.

How can that be? Mommy wonders. The doors are locked, the business is closed, no one else is inside. Was there an intruder?

Mommy goes to take a look. She checks the hallway and the nearby rooms. There is no exit and anyone coming or going would be visibly seen, but she doesn't see anyone. They are alone in the building, but she believes her daughter. The child is too traumatized for her to believe otherwise.

The only other explanation for her daughter's fright is that the child saw an apparition.

That logic may be something to debate, but this is the Taube Museum of Art, which has a history of supernatural activity. It wouldn't be tough to believe that a ghost, only moments before, had appeared to her daughter.

Guests and staff over the years have reported a number of strange occurrences in the building that is known today as the Taube Museum of Art, located at 2 Main Street North. Activity here includes the sounds of walking when no one else is there to make the foot-slap noises, the feelings of being watched, and, more unnerving, the manifestation of apparitions. Besides the little girl who apparently saw a figure, a person on staff said she once saw the phantom of a man whom she chased around the gallery, at first thinking it was a real person who had trespassed after hours but finding, instead, it was an ephemeral being—yet it appeared just as plainly as if it were a living mortal.

Unnerving? Perhaps for most people. But for those who know the Taube, chalk it up to just another day at the museum.

Executive Director Rachel Alfaro, who had been working at the museum for about three-and-a-half years by the time we spoke on July 14, 2022, said she has never experienced paranormal activity in the building. But she doesn't discount the stories. After all, it was her daughter who came running back from the hallway with fright on her face, and tears running down her cheeks, because she had seen a ghostly visage.

The incident happened in December 2021 during renovations of the facility. Some might claim it is the renovations that cause the hauntings, but paranormal activity here has been going on for a long time.

Wendy Kimble, a paranormal investigator but also a volunteer at the museum since 1997, said she has heard stories from many people over the years who claim to have had their own experience with the paranormal while in the building.

Her inclination to the paranormal—and her connection to the museum as a volunteer—makes the Taube one of her favorite haunts, literally, in Minot. It was here that she had what she described as her most "intense" episode with the ghostly. It happened like this:

> At around 5:30 on a Monday afternoon, after instructing students in a class about art, she waited for parents to arrive to pick up their kids. Most of them had left on time, but two of the students were still awaiting their parents' arrival when Kimble saw a man walk down the stairs. Thinking it was a parent, she told the girls to grab their belongings and get ready to leave. She then approached the man with a greeting. He never said a word but, instead, looked at her—or looked past her,

she couldn't tell which—and all of sudden jerked right, went past her, and headed into the gallery.

Kimble followed, telling the man the museum was closed, that he had to vacate the building. The man, still mum, outpaced her and veered around a bend.

Thinking she could cut him off the other way, she went a different direction, but the man was nowhere to be seen.

Kimble said there was no way he could have exited without her noticing. It wasn't until then that she realized the figure she had been chasing was not a flesh-and-blood human. It was a spirit entity. But she swears to this day that the personage she saw looked as real as any human does.

But nope, apparently this man was all spirit.

This may have been Kimble's most intense experience with the paranormal, but it is not the only thing she has experienced at the Taube. She said that ever since she started in her position with the building more than two decades ago, she has experienced such activities as hearing phantom footfalls and feelings as if she was being watched.

Paranormal investigators rely on equipment to detect spirits, but they also rely on their intuition. Some people may discount this as fancy feelings or self-created notions, but the natural senses—which alert us to danger or even if someone is behind us—should not be ignored. "The gallery manager, or the executive director at the time, had never really thought much about it," Kimble said. "She had heard footsteps and experienced other stuff going on and just kind of brushed it off."

Another story Kimble shared about the Taube relates back to children and their experiences in the building. She said museum staff often do tours with school and Scout groups, taking visitors to the different floors, showing them the museum's exhibits and its many pieces of art. An upper level holds the facility's permanent collection and serves as space for the artist in residence.

Alfaro describes the place like this: "Roughly every four to six weeks we change out our exhibits. We have two main exhibit spaces on two floors. There's an upstairs and a downstairs. And then there's a third floor as well, and that is occasionally open to the public, but not all of the time, which is where our artist-in-residence space is. It's a working space on the third floor; and then the main level and the lower floor are exhibit spaces, and on the ground or lower level are two classrooms."

Kimble said that in about one of every three tours she has hosted, children will invariably stop to point or ask questions about who the person is in the upper level when it is unoccupied. One time she brought her young granddaughter with her to work. "We were going upstairs to talk to the executive director and she froze on the steps," Kimble related. She urged her granddaughter: "'Let's go. We gotta go talk to this lady up here.' She was like no, no, no, no. 'You're okay, I say. Come on.'" Kimble tried coaxing her, but the child looked up at that room with fright on her face. Finally, Kimble relented. "'You don't have to go up there.'" Her granddaughter eased after that.

The building now known as the Taube hasn't always been a museum. It had another life as the home of Union National Bank, founded in 1909, which resided in the building from 1963, after a series of events led it to various locations during the ensuing decades, until 1997 when it became the Taube Museum of Art.

There's a bit of history to the museum organization as well.

Founded by the Minot Art Association in 1970, the Minot Art Gallery was initially located in a home off Highway 83 North before moving, in 1978, to the Ward County Historical Society building at the North Dakota State Fairgrounds, east of Minot. A few years later, it was once again relocated to another Historical Society building at the Fairgrounds, the J. E. Harmon House, where it operated until 1997 when it moved to its final home in the Union National Bank building. It was then that the building, not a bank any longer, received its new name. Due to generous support from Lillian and Coleman Taube, the Minot Art Gallery was changed to the Lillian and Coleman Taube Museum of Art and, today, is one of the staples of the Minot community.

The facility, all three stories of it, showcases the work of artists, facilitates painting and other educational classes, and holds public events throughout the year. Exhibits, which the museum changes about every six weeks or so, Alfaro said, are supported by the North Dakota Council on the Arts. It's free to visit the museum, but donations are always welcome.

Indeed, the museum is a fine addition to the Minot community—a downtown that has both a colorful history and seems rife with paranormal activity.

Minot's founding in 1886 was perhaps unintentional, but its creation has had a significant impact on the state ever since. It was originally founded as a tent town when the construction of the Great Northern Railroad, owned by Jim Hill, stopped here for the winter, partly due to problems constructing a trestle over Gassman Coulee. As if by magic, a tent town rapidly came into existence, giving Minot its moniker "The Magic City."

Minot itself, which was incorporated in 1887, received its name from railroad investor Henry James Minot. As a new century approached, Minot continued to blossom, experiencing all of the booms and busts of other western-type towns as it grew into its own place. It also experienced the wiles of Mother Nature, such as a devastating flood from the Souris River in 1969. With help from the Army Corps of Engineers, the river's run through the city was altered and a number of flood control measures were installed—perhaps serving as a little more magic that humans, as we learned long ago from the beaver, knew would alter the course of a river.

But while Minot is more favorably known as the Magic City, its downtown also has another nickname in its history: Little Chicago.

It is rumored that downtown Minot received a lot of attention during prohibition in the 1920s and received the moniker "Little Chicago," for the high crime activity that once loomed here, including, as rumored, Al Capone operating shady business dealings in the area. One didn't have to journey far to witness all sorts of lascivious activity, including drugs and prostitution; they were around every corner. They were even underground; tunnels were used to transport nefarious substances and feed the criminal enterprises.

Today, a century since the Roaring Twenties, the downtown area retains a bit of those bygone days with a number of bars that cater to the public, only without the more devious vices known in Little Chicago's time.

The word "Magic" today is indeed a better term for this vibrant city, which has an active air force base, progressive university, innovative business community, impressive sports and recreation arenas, and a number of other opportunities for families and visitors to enjoy. Unlike what it may have been in the past, it is a family-friendly community.

But apparently one that is not without its ghosts.

Kimble and her team at Paranormal Investigators of North Dakota, who have investigated many of the buildings downtown, said the whole downtown area is haunted. With such an interesting and colorful history that is Minot, how can it be otherwise?

ART, WINE, ORBS, AND A SPIRIT NAMED KAREN

URBAN WINERY, MINOT

Numerous orbs appear as if they are floating up from the floor. Alarms go off when no human is there to provoke the sensors. A shrill, unnerving screech is caught on a recorder when no human being is around. And a spirit believed to be a former prostitute named Karen has been detected in the building that today serves as Urban Winery, a hip and welcoming spot in downtown Minot.

Karen seems attached to the business's owner, Eric Hansen, who opened the winery in June 2017. He was told this by a medium who came to investigate the premises after a number of paranormal occurrences transpired in the building. Ever since, Hansen sets out a bouquet of flowers every couple of weeks for Karen. They sit on his desk, where most of the activity seems to resonate.

This is where orbs have been recorded floating upward in a gush of frenzy—a dozen or more moving in unified excitement as if hosting their own party. A video of moving orbs, along with others captured by recording, can be seen on Urban Winery's Facebook page, where Hansen posts them from time to time.

Hansen said he can't quite explain the activity that he's experienced over the past few years, but he doesn't believe anything in the building is malicious in nature. The only thing that might be found unnerving is that, sometimes, female guests will complain about feeling watched by someone, or something, unseen in the women's restroom. The history of the building may account for those feelings, according to Hansen. The building was once used as a brothel. He was told by one medium who visited the building that a number of spirits still linger on the premises, both male and female, including the female spirit the investigator said was named Karen. The unnerving feelings that some guests experience in the restroom could be from the perving eyes of male spirits beyond the veil who once worked here as johns, managing the prostitutes.

Other than those reported feelings—nothing concrete—most of the experiences have been benign, but one sent goose pimples crawling up Hansen's back.

At about 6 p.m. on a Sunday, Hansen left his place of business and headed to a local watering hole to unwind for the day. While there, he started getting a number of text messages alerting him that his shop's security cameras were detecting movement. But no one was in the building. No one with flesh and blood, anyway. "My security system will send me a short little video—a five-second video, sometimes it's a ten-second video—of any activity that will trigger that motion. It was strange how it was happening. I would get a video text like every two or three minutes, but I couldn't see anything on the video. I didn't have the sound on, I was just looking at the video, but at one point I put my headphones in and I caught a blood-curdling scream. But nobody was in the building and it freaked me out."

He said that at one point it sounded like two different voices were making the unnerving ruckus. One voice, according to the recording, sounded like it was saying "no," the other, toward the end of the recording, was "a different male voice screaming," he explained. "That's the one and only time I've caught any audio. And again, there was no one there, no visual of anything that would have tripped the security camera. . . . But I continued to get video alerts, and pretty soon I started seeing these little orbs. They're beautiful the way they track through the frame; it looks almost like there's a kid blowing bubbles, but the bubbles move with purpose. They don't just hang and go up or down. It looks like they're going from one doorway to another doorway."

After this experience, Hansen didn't waste any time contacting those who might be able to give him answers for the strange activity in his building. He reached out to Wendy Kimble of PIND and within a day or two they arrived to conduct a preliminary investigation. Using equipment including a FLIR (forward-looking infrared) camera, which uses thermal technology to sense infrared radiation, they were able to catch some phantom impressions.

They said to place it [the camera] in the area where you think most of the activity is happening. I placed it in that area where the desk is and the area that seems to catch most of the orbs—and in the recording of the FLIR camera, you can see my footsteps as I pick up my foot and walk forward. You can see my step behind me go from warm to almost disappear. While I'm into the next step, that footprint seems to disappear. I put the box down and suddenly there were two footprints, blue footprints right next to mine. . . . The footprints stayed in that same spot, just a foot or so away from where I was standing. My footprints disappeared, but those footprints, the blue footprints, stayed there for, I don't know, ten or fifteen minutes. It was just weird, and then suddenly they were gone.

Hansen feels that these experiences and others have helped fine-tune his own spiritual senses. "I believe this is why children seem to be very open to things that happen spiritually; with them the veil is much thinner," he said. "When we're children, our imaginations are much more awake, and I think as we are tasked with different activities and pushed in certain doctrines and disciplines, we kind of get away from the vibrational alignment of things that are spiritual. We get away from nature and miss the stuff that's a lot deeper."

Hansen, a genteel man with an artist's gift, has decorated Urban Winery with all sorts of self-created artwork of celebrities. Walking into his place of business is like returning to a place you've known before, greeted by friends and good wine. One of the walls displays fine works of the musician Prince—a fitting subject for Hansen's creativity, since both he and Prince Rogers Nelson hail from Minneapolis—as do many other celebrities.

Another neat thing about the winery is that it allows customers to bottle their own wine. They can come for taste tests, select their flavors, bottle it, and leave it with Hansen during the fermenting process before returning a few weeks later to pick it up. This serves as a special gift for those about to be wed. They can literally create their own wine for their wedding.

If you like wine and art, Urban Winery, located at 6 North Main Suite 103, is a must-see stop the next time you're in Minot. Just be sure to also ask about the other kinds of spirits, including a ghost named Karen, that seem to linger here.

CREEPY GOINGS-ON AT A COMIC BOOK SHOP

ORIGINAL COMICS AND COLLECTIBLES, MINOT

For most people, it's all fun and games at a comic book shop until the ghosts show up. But for a paranormal investigative team, the fun ramps up another notch whenever they make contact with the spirits at Original Comics and Collectibles.

The shop is a favorite haunt—literally—for the team of Paranormal Investigators of North Dakota (whom I've already mentioned several times in previous stories). It's where they often go to experience activity from the unseen world. And it's where they take potential new team members to see how they fit with current members and how they react to paranormal disturbances. They come here, to this shop at 10 1st Street Northwest, because it is such an active place.

Ghosts aside, it's a fun shop anyway, with its 1980s and 1990s collectibles.

The building has existed for decades, possibly built in the 1940s. It has been many things over the years—starting with being the first drive-thru bank in Minot. It was later a drive-thru cleaners and an OSHA training site before it sprang to life as a comic shop in 2017.

This is a special shop for Stephanie Pinkey, co-founder of PIND, for it is her husband, Will Pinkey, who owns this store. It sells all sorts of fan memorabilia from Star Wars and He-Man, secondhand video games, and Legos, among many other items. It is a fun store to browse—and for Pinkey and her team, it is a fun place to tap into the paranormal.

The one-story building does have a basement, and it is there, at the lower level, where an entrance to Minot's underground tunnels can be found. It was in the tunnel cavity where Stephanie and her team once saw a figure, whom they presumed to have been a spirit, though they do not know this for sure. It was crouched down, wearing light clothing, and once it finally moved to stand up it seemed to vanish from their view.

More common disturbances the team has experienced at the facility are phantom footsteps that seem to move from one room to the next, as if someone were walking from room to room. During one investigation during a candidate tryout at the old shop, Wendy Kimble said a group of about four females were in the middle of a room when suddenly the energy of the room began to change. It wasn't only the investigative team that was in the room any longer; there also were unseen entities with them, and whatever or whoever they were, they seemed to like the women. Some of the females on the team started feeling weird sensations, as if unseen hands were touching their backs near their bra straps. One woman's bra strap became unclasped by the unseen hands of a mischievous spirit who wasn't afraid to be flagrantly flirtatious with its prank.

Pinkey said her husband hasn't talked a lot about what he may have experienced in the shop, as he sits more on the skeptic side of the fence. "Wendy calls him a muggle," Stephanie said with a chuckle, referring to the non-wizards of the Harry Potter universe, "because he doesn't really believe." One time, however, he joined the team during an investigation and saw equipment go off by itself. "He was like, what the heck is that?" Stephanie said. "It scared the crap out of him. It was funny."

The conclusion as to why the comic shop is so active, Stephanie said, is likely because it sits near a river and railroad tracks that are still used today. "Normally, when a place like a railroad track or river that has constant energy like that, the activity of a place ramps up," she explained.

"Which is pretty much the whole town of Minot," Wendy added, explaining why there are so many buildings in the downtown area with a haunted history. Most of the buildings downtown have some sort of paranormal activity associated with them, she said. Which makes Minot, especially its downtown, a favorite haunted site for the investigative team. And among the top favorites is Original Comics and Collectibles.

Check it out the next time you're in town. It's a fun place to visit, ghosts or not. How can it not be with Star Wars and He-Man and other collectibles? It's understandable why the ghosts might like this place, too.

THE HAUNTED HARVEY

HARVEY PUBLIC LIBRARY, HARVEY

If a spirit haunts a public library, does that mean it likes to read?

No, this isn't the setup to a joke but, rather, a question as to why at least one spirit seems to haunt the Harvey Public Library in the small town of Harvey, North Dakota, located in the central region of the state between Valley City to the southeast and Minot to the northwest. But once you dig a little deeper, you realize there are other reasons the spirit of a woman may be haunting the site. Those who have had encounters with her even call her by name: "Sophie."

If the spirit in the Harvey Library is indeed that belonging to Sophia Eberlein-Benz, her history may very well be tied to the haunting.

Russian-born Sophia emigrated to the United States, settling in North Dakota with her first husband, businessman Hugo Eberlein, with whom she had two daughters. Hugo died in 1928. Sophia later decided to once again tie the knot, this time to a man named Jacob Bentz, a local plumber. As time would tell, however, it was a decision that eventually ended in ruin.

The two-year marriage wasn't ideal from the start, but things got worse after a late-night argument when things turned tragic. In the early morning hours of

October 2, 1931, Bentz brutally bludgeoned his wife to death in their home. His plan, apparently, was to make it look like Sophia died in a car crash, but one of Sophia's daughters visited the house and she became suspicious. She found traces of blood, and her step-father's story just didn't seem to make sense to her. She notified the authorities of what she had found, and police investigated the scene, becoming more suspicious of Bentz as time went on. Bentz eventually confessed to the murder, telling authorities in the very room where he committed the despicable crime how he had killed his wife.

The accounts tell this story: Bentz said he had struck his wife with a hammer while she readied for bed shortly after 1 a.m., according to what he told the judge at the time. He said they were in a heated argument, which turned his supposed love to hate. "I love her yet. I lost my head when we argued. I intended to kill myself too," he told the judge. "I felt so sorry. It wouldn't have happened if we hadn't quarreled." (Some reports say he struck his wife while she was sleeping.)

His actions afterward, however, enforce the belief that he very much played the part of the criminal. Instead of feeling immediate remorse for injuring his wife and calling the authorities to help her, he instead placed her body in the family car, apparently while she was still alive, and drove into a ditch some eight miles away. He thought this duplicitous act would make it appear as if his wife died in an automobile accident. To further enhance the claim, he set fire to the vehicle, telling authorities it had caught fire when it plunged about ten feet into its resting place. Authorities, however, discovered that the evidence pointed to the contrary and concluded that Bentz himself was the one who set fire to the vehicle.

Initial reports, however, believed Bentz's story. Two paragraphs related the story in a report about local deaths in the October 2, 1931 issue of *The Bismarck Tribune*.

"Mrs. Sophie Bentz Burned to Death as Crash Pinions Her in Auto," reads the headline. The story reads, in part: "Mrs. Sophie Everlein Bentz, 45, Harvey, burned to death when the automobile which she was driving plunged into a ditch and burst into flames. Her husband, Jacob Bentz, was unhurt. The enclosed car left country road and followed a V-shaped ditch until it came to a standstill. Mrs. Bentz was driving and the crash pinioned her in the machine. Fire broke out and despite efforts of Mr. Bentz to save her, she was burned to death."

While Bentz claimed it was the argument that led to his rash, life-altering decisions, authorities believed his motive was premeditated and planned with a financial purpose in mind. Bentz later told authorities that after he struck his wife, he called their insurance company and asked that policies for both him and his wife be written for $5,000. "Mrs. Bentz was reputed to have an estate valued at approximately $75,000, but through pre-nuptial agreement, Bentz was to receive little of her estate in event of death" (*Tribune*). While Bentz stuck to his claim, "authorities believed his motive was to 'cash in' on the insurance policy he had purchased after his attack."

For his evil act he was sentenced to life in prison. Announcing his confession, *The Bismarck Tribune*, in its Tuesday, October 6, 1931 issue, published the account with the screaming headline "CONFESSES HAMMER MURDER." In the article to which that headline ties, a smaller headline read: "HARVEY MAN SENT TO PRISON AFTER CONFESSING CRIME: Pleads Guilty to First Degree Murder in District Court Here."

"Six hours after he recounted to authorities how he struck his wife with a claw-hammer and burned her body in the family automobile," the article began, "Jacob Bentz, 49, Harvey plumber, began serving a life term in the state penitentiary here Monday night," reported the major newspaper of Bismark, the town wherein he died in 1944.

Sophia was laid to rest at Sunnyside Cemetery in Harvey. Her final resting place can be found along row 14, in section 3 of the burial grounds. A simple grave marker, without her last name, reads: SOPHIE—1889–1931.

But something apparently has remained behind in the place where the evil deed took place. The home where Sophia was murdered sat where the Harvey Library is located today. It is said that the library opened in 1990 on the anniversary of Sophia's funeral, fifty-nine years after she had died.

In his fine book titled *The Best of Dakota Mysteries and Oddities*, William Jackson postulates that it could very well be Sophia's spirit that lingers at the library.

While Bentz's spirit seems to have gone to the great beyond to await judgment for his evil deed, Sophia's spirit, on the other hand, if Jackson is correct, may not have left the property of her earthly demise. It has been speculated that the strange happenings at the library are caused by Sophia's spirit—or Sophie, as library staff call her. Some of the activities reported at the library are books and other items placed in plain sight that inexplicably go missing—only to turn up later when it was obvious no one had set them where they were found—and lights that turn off and on by themselves. Cold spots and apparitions have also been reported at the library.

These strange occurrences, and others like them, have happened so often and have been witnessed by so many people that the Harvey Public Library usually turns up on lists that mention alleged haunted hotspots in North Dakota. I reached out to the library several times, and was briefly told by one library staff member that she had made peace with Sophie. But other attempts to follow up or contact the library about the stories received no response.

The library remains one of the popular sites on North Dakota's paranormal lists, perhaps because of the gruesome story associated with the property it was built upon. But reporters from other media outlets, who had better luck speaking with folks at the library than I did, seem to tell stories that suggest that Sophie, or whatever entity has disturbed the facility, is real and not folklore or legend.

According to one article in the *Grand Forks Herald*, published October 30, 2009, the library had the electrical wiring looked at but electricians have "never solved the mystery of the library's fluttering lights." This and the other strange happenings here left "library workers [to] wonder if the place isn't home to a bookworm from the beyond."

THE BISMARCK REGION

THE MANY HAUNTS OF NORTH DAKOTA'S CAPITAL CITY

BISMARCK

Bismarck, which lies in Burleigh County in the south-central part of the state, was founded in 1872—but it didn't always have the same name as a famous sunken ship. Originally, it was named Edwinton, after Edwin L. Johnson, a proponent of the transcontinental railway. The name was short-lived, however, and it received the name of Bismarck just a year later in 1873.

And no, it wasn't really named after the German battleship *Bismarck*, which was sunk by the British on May 27, 1941, near France in the North Atlantic, long after the city received its name. But the city's name does have German roots. It was named—perhaps with a financial ploy in mind—after German chancellor Otto von Bismarck. It was hoped that using his name would attract German investment in the railway, which seemed to work. That same year, the railway did indeed arrive, further enhancing the community and its growth. It coincided with the discovery of gold in South Dakota's Black Hills, and Bismarck became an outfitting center for prospectors. Nine years later, in 1883, the capital of Dakota Territory was moved from Yankton, in present-day South Dakota, to Bismarck, where it stayed after the Territory was split into two states in 1889.

Mandan, located farther south in Morton County across the Missouri River from Bismarck, was also settled in 1873 and named after the Mandan tribe. Both cities have histories tied to the railroad, and both were visited by Lewis and Clark during their Corps of Discovery Expedition in 1804–1805.

Today, both Mandan and Bismarck are progressive communities, pleasant places to visit, and boast an array of activities to pursue both indoors and outside. And according to at least one paranormal investigator, they also are communities that are deep-rooted in the paranormal.

For Caedmon Marx, the paranormal has never been too far away. Perhaps it is in his genes. According to Marx, possibly his mother but for sure his grandmother and great-aunt on his mother's side have strong psychic and paranormal sensibilities. Marx himself saw his first apparition when he was twelve years old at the Custer House at Fort Abraham Lincoln State Park. By age nineteen, he had become one of the world's youngest demonologists. The latter hints that he has had experiences with the darker side of the supernatural.

He speaks cautiously about his experiences, saying how people must be careful when they approach things unseen. You never know what you might pick up on a ghost hunt, for instance, and he says people should think twice before messing with a Ouija board. They are doors into the darker recesses of the netherworld. The consequence of opening those doors is that you cannot control what may come through. Often, it is not what the daring paranormal enthusiast intended.

Marx said investigating the paranormal can be frightening, but if approached cautiously and carefully, it can lend itself to finding answers as well as additional questions.

Marx has traveled to many places in the state to investigate the paranormal, but mostly he stays closer to home, where he investigates both commercial and residential properties. There are plenty of places in Bismarck and the surrounding area that keeps him busy. The state's capital is a haunted city, he said, where many places seem to be disturbed by the paranormal.

Like most paranormal investigators, Marx tries to debunk the activity, trying to find rational explanations as to why a business or homeowner might be hearing or sensing something in their abode. He is often successful at this endeavor, showing that not every strange sound a resident hears is an echo from the unseen world; sometimes it is just the house settling. He said, for instance, that when people were sent home to work during the height of the coronavirus pandemic, many of them, not being familiar with the regular noises of their homes during the day, were all of a sudden there to experience what to them may have sounded like paranormal activity. However, there are other times when the evidence obtained points directly and convincingly at activity beyond this mortal realm.

As for the reason Bismarck may be one of North Dakota's most haunted places, he offers a couple of suggestions. For one, he said that wood from Fort Abraham Lincoln, which is steeped in history, was used to construct some of the buildings early on. Could spirits have attached themselves to those particles and followed them to their new construction sites? For another, Bismarck lies near the Missouri River. Water creates energy, and in paranormal circles it is believed that spirits need energy to manifest themselves. Could the river be supplying needed energy for the alleged entities in and around Bismarck, allowing them to make themselves known to today's current residents?

These are theories, of course, but they are not off-kilter to the common beliefs of those who study the paranormal.

Marx did not want to share the names of businesses or homeowners he has worked with to keep their privacy, but said—based on some of the experiences he has had while investigating places in Bismarck, Mandan, and the surrounding area—that if people experience disturbances in their abodes, they should not panic. "There are many different reasons something might be happening. A strange noise could be just a little maintenance that needs to be done on the house," he said. "And so before really jumping into the paranormal side of 'my house is haunted,' look into those other things first."

However, if it is real activity, there are reasons for that, too. Did something unseen attach itself to an object or even the property? Did something follow you or a family member home? Have you experimented with a Ouija board or other tools that open doors to the dark side? In rare cases, it might not be a haunting at all, at least not in the traditional sense, but rather activity from psychic abilities that the person might be repressing, deep emotions that could actually create their own haunting. Some people, in essence, could be haunting themselves.

"Definitely one of the prevailing theories on what a poltergeist actually is, comes from someone who is gifted, who is repressing a lot of emotion," he said. "That is not healthy." It is commonly believed that poltergeist activity often happens around young people during their pubescence, especially girls.

In essence, he said there are "layers upon layers" of the paranormal and why activity might be happening. He also said different religions have different views on such activity. His take: "If we're thinking about the paranormal, we can't prescribe to one religious theory, like the Catholics are all right and everyone else is wrong," he said. "Native American cultures speak of skin walkers, shapeshifting entities that wreak havoc on their victims. Different cultures and religions have their own take on otherworldly beings. . . . Those are actual entities, such as the skin walkers, and they may not really be prescribed to your religion. You have to really open your mind, definitely, when working in this field."

One thing is for sure, according to Marx: Bismarck is definitely a haunted city.

GHOSTLY POLITICIANS

THE OLD GOVERNOR'S MANSION, BISMARCK

Politicians and government leaders, once busy as mortals trying to keep their parties happy, do not always find peace once they pass from this mortal existence.

That's not to say these restless spirits were bad people on Earth, but more likely that, as spirits, they find it hard to be out of touch with their earthly work and constituents once they leave their mortal bodies. Sometimes, they come back to check on things.

Could such be the case with the spirit of early North Dakota governor Frank Briggs?

When Briggs died in the master bedroom of his stately Victorian-style mansion in 1898, little did he know that something of him would remain at the property. But according to the stories, that is exactly what seems to have happened.

Located at 320 East Avenue B in Bismarck, the nineteenth-century two-story, five-bedroom home—large for its time—first belonged to Asa Fisher, a banker and wholesale liquor dealer, who built the house in 1884. But after occupying the house for only nine years, he sold it in 1893 to the state of North Dakota, and a few years later it became the official residence of the state's next twenty or so governors.

Briggs was the first governor to occupy the Victorian homestead. He was also the only one to die at the house while in office, thus lending to the assumption that it is his spirit who haunts the place. The governor was only thirty-eight years old on the day of his inauguration on January 6, 1897, and only served for a little more than a year and a half before dying at the stately house on August 9, 1898, from tuberculosis.

Briggs, born in Minneapolis on September 15, 1858, worked in the newspaper and real estate industries before pursuing a life in politics. His first step took him to Morton County, where he served as treasurer, and then later as state auditor, before being elected to the North Dakota governor's post in 1896. He was an active legislator and the fifth person to hold the executive office in North Dakota. During his administration, he was able to see a railway law passed that regulated the transportation of passengers and freight and a general revenue law, which held many of Briggs's provisions.

Unexpectedly, sickness struck, and he went to bed never to recover from his illness. After he passed, Briggs's body was returned to the North Star State, where he was laid to rest at the Howard Lake Cemetery in Howard Lake, Minnesota. His lieutenant governor, Joseph M. Devine, filled Briggs's term after his passing.

Since Briggs's time, more than twenty other governors have taken up residence at the state mansion. But it is believed that it is Briggs's spirit that has never left. Most of the ghost stories started after about 1907, when then-governor Burke ordered renovations of the property. The large attic was redone, becoming part playroom for the children; another portion served as quarters for the butler, Tom Lee. Apparently, Lee began experiencing paranormal activity after he started sleeping in the attic and refused to do so when the family wasn't home. It is unclear what truth this story about Lee holds, but that is the rumor.

Phantom footsteps have been heard in several places of the house, curtains and doors have been seen to move of their own volition, and EVPs have been caught during paranormal investigations at the site.

Wendy Kimble and Stephanie Pinkey and their team investigated the governor's mansion, and said they had a lot of activity that night. They had the music box in the front entrance, a Bobo Bear stuffed animal in the children's room upstairs—both the box and stuffed animal have sensors—and a REM Pod in the governor's room. "We had non-stop activity all night," Kimble said, noting that the music box played when it detected a presence move into the room; the REM Pod also went off when team members asked questions, implying that an unseen entity was replying through the technology.

"Stephanie and I had tons of reactions in the children's room, the playroom upstairs. The Bobo Bear would go off nonstop. We always try and do this very scientifically. Is it the batteries that is causing it to go off? Is a wire messed up, especially with it going off that often? Maybe there's something wrong with it. And so we moved positions, changed it around." But it kept detecting an unseen presence in the room with them. "Whoever was in there really enjoyed that bear," Kimble said, noting she believes Governor Briggs's spirit made an appearance the night they investigated. "I feel he was definitely there that night," she said.

Also, a member of the historical committee who was with them during the investigation told the team an eerie story. The night Briggs died, he was seen standing on his balcony overlooking the downtown fires that were raging at the time. But, as the staff discovered, the young governor was actually in bed, deceased. Other stories are not so ghostly, saying the governor watched the fires while resting on a sofa on the mansion's porch.

A new governor's mansion was built in 1960, and the old Victorian mansion has since become a historic site and museum, operated by the North Dakota State Historical Society. When visiting the site today, it is as if one steps back in time to North Dakota's early days when Briggs was governor. The décor, from furnishings to wallpaper, resembles that in play during Briggs's stay at the house. Maybe that is why his spirit has remained—he seems to be attached to this place where he lived and died while serving as North Dakota's fifth chief executive.

LAYERS OF HISTORY AND HAUNTINGS

FORT ABRAHAM LINCOLN AND THE CUSTER HOUSE, MANDAN

George Armstrong Custer, a complex and interesting individual, has been called many things: frontiersman, patriot, courageous war hero, martyr . . . coward, despot, and racist. He remains a controversial figure, but no matter how one may view the famous general, his history is, if nothing else, interesting. Custer was by all accounts a brave—if not brazen—individual who led many skirmishes that culminated in his own death at the battle of the Little Bighorn in 1876.

Born December 5, 1839, in New Rumley, Ohio, Custer spent much of his childhood living with his half-sister and brother-in-law in Michigan. Eventually, with the help of a state legislator, he was able to attend the US Military Academy at West Point, setting him on his future career path as a soldier and, later, general.

This is surprising, perhaps, since he didn't do so well in academics. A person doesn't need to excel at math to be a good soldier, of course, but one does have to know how to take orders, something that Custer also struggled with at West Point. He was known to be a lazy student, got himself into trouble a number of times, and came close to being expelled more than once. He received a number of demerits and graduated last in his class.

But his career was not to be in academics (though he did write a best-selling book); rather it was on the battlefield. It seemed as if fate foretold this early on and paved his way to success. The political and societal climate of the time helped further cement his journey. Custer graduated in 1861, when the flames of civil war were being stoked, and just a few weeks after he received his diploma, he was sent to fight in the Battle of Bull Run. He may not have caught his teachers' attention in school but he seemed to excel on the battlefield, and he caught the attention of General George McClellan. Custer served with McClellan in the Peninsula Campaign a year later, which further cemented his reputation as a brave and talented soldier.

These conflicts were only the beginning of young Custer's military career that would span numerous conflicts and years. Some of the battles he would later fight included those at Gettysburg and Appomattox, and along the way he rose in rank, which helped cement his legacy as a war-hardened frontiersman.

But, for now, there was one battle that loomed. Custer escaped with his life during the Civil War, but his fate lay just on the horizon at a place called the Little Bighorn.

FORT ABRAHAM LINCOLN

There's a historic fort in Mandan, North Dakota, that at first glance might seem like it wouldn't have anything to do with the famous 1800s general. After all, the fort is named after America's first assassinated president, not the plains warrior who was struck down on the northern prairie during an ill-conceived and gratuitous conflict.

This fort, of course, is Fort Abraham Lincoln, one of North Dakota's most famous state parks "and definitely the most steeped in Custeriana," writes Jeff Barnes, author of the notable *The Great Plains Guide to Custer: 85 Forts & Other Sites* (181).

Like Custer, Fort Abraham Lincoln has an interesting history. To tell it, we must start with knowing that the Mandan tribe, in about 1575, first established the area with a village of their own. About eighty-five earthen lodges were built on a sloping plain near what today is called the Missouri River. Because of its sloped angle, it was called Miti O-pa-e-resh, or On-a-Slant Village, which was home to about 1,500 people. The citizens there hunted and harvested and enjoyed life on the plains—until smallpox plagued the village and sent the Mandan fleeing in 1781.

Leave it to Meriwether Lewis and William Clark to happen upon the village a little more than two decades later, in 1804. The site, however, didn't get a new lease on life until about seventy years later with the approach of the Northern Pacific Railroad.

Barnes, in his savvy book about historic forts and other sites on the plains, retells the coming of age of Fort Abraham Lincoln:

> The Northern Pacific approached Bismarck in 1872 and needed a fort for protecting its work crews. A site was selected across the Missouri and downstream from the town on a bluff overlooking the river. It was named Fort McKeen for Col. Henry McKeen, killed at the Civil War battle of Cold Harbor.

General Sheridan visited the fort later that year and didn't like the site selected. He ordered further development to take place on the flats below the bluff and called for cavalry to become a major part of the fort. Finally, he renamed the post Fort Abraham Lincoln in honor of the nation's assassinated president.

When completed, the Northern Pacific would be the second transcontinental route after the Union Pacific, but it was going into unexplored territory that hosted aggressive tribes who were more resistant to the white man. The army would play a major role in the construction of the route and Fort Abraham Lincoln became its home on the northern plains. (176)

Custer and his Seventh Cavalry spent time at Fort Abraham, and it became known as "the Custer Post," according to Barnes (177). It was from here where he dispatched his soldiers, sometimes leaving the fort undefended for periods of time while they were away to the Black Hills and other points to track Native Americans. And it was here, in the home he shared with his wife, Libbie, and their children, that Custer remained when his book, *My Life on the Plains*, was released to wide acclaim.

The fort, with a growing history of its own, remained after Custer's demise on June 25, 1876, at the Battle of the Little Bighorn. It became a state park in 1907 and is the oldest state park in North Dakota.

Today, visitors can explore the culture and history of the native Mandan tribe by seeing reconstructed earthen lodges that resemble the original village abodes, and they can discover what life was like as a frontier soldier by visiting the blockhouses and furnished barracks and participate in living history by touring the commanding officer's quarters.

Visitors also can learn more about the Custer family and their home here on the plains at the secluded fort. The Custer House, indeed, is a popular destination at the park and has a few paranormal stories associated with it.

This is not the original Custer home, but in 2019 the park celebrated thirty years since the Custer house was rebuilt. The original Custer house, built in 1873, burned down a year later, in 1874, prompting the need for a second house. Libbie and Custer lived at the fort from 1873 until his death in 1876, and their new home was dismantled in 1894. Almost a hundred years later, a group formed the Abraham Lincoln Foundation and built the replica home in 1989.

"The house has been refurnished as it was in Custer's time and is open to the public for living history tours," according to a July 22, 2014, article in *The Bismarck Tribune*. An image with the story shows a reenactment of a period battle. "Interpreters dressed in period costumes guide visitors through the house which today is mostly filled with recreation pieces of furniture, dishes and clothing, but there are a number of articles on display that were actually owned by the Custers." When coming upon the house, a sign greets visitors with the words: "WELCOME TO FORT ABRAHAM LINCOLN, THE YEAR IS 1875."

And indeed, it does feel like a time warp, as if you've stepped across a barrier to another time and place that seems both familiar and distant. The ghosts, besides any literal ones that may roam here, speak the unspoken words of being in a place where history feels as if it is reaching out, tickling the senses and spurring thoughts of what used to be. *Remember us,* those distant memories say. *You're so busy today. Remember what life was like when . . .*

As for the more traditional ghosts, those of the paranormal kind, there allegedly are some of those here, too.

GHOSTS OF THE CUSTER POST

Stories have circulated for years about paranormal activity at the Custer House, from apparitions that have made themselves known to phantom voices and other noises that have been heard in the supposedly haunted abode. According to an October 26, 2021, report by KX News, some of the tour guides have claimed to have heard the snap of billiard balls in the game room, a very common sound, they have said, according to the report.

More frightening is the apparition of a woman, who appears in the morning or evening dressed in a dark gown. It has been said that this spirit figure may very well be the wife of General Custer, Libbie, who took care of their home. Libbie, who outlived her husband by fifty-seven years, stayed true to his memory after his death. Emerging from the Civil War as a battle hero, Custer was branded a hero, and as his fame grew, Libbie often shared the spotlight with him. She kept the hero worship alive in the three books she wrote during her lifetime.

Why her spirit would follow to the new home, built in 1989 as a replica of her original home on the plains, is anyone's guess. But one assumption is that she is attracted to the familiarity of the house.

Caedmon Marx, a paranormal investigator and demonologist with the Haunted Plains Paranormal Society, which he founded, said this might very well be the case.

Marx has a special connection to Fort Abraham Lincoln and the Custer House. It was here, in Custer's replicated abode, where, up close and personal, he had his first experience—not his last—with an apparition. It happened during a school field trip to the site with his classmates at the age of twelve. While touring the house, Marx said he saw a woman dressed in period clothing that vanished from his view soon after noticing her. The woman, he found out later after seeing an old-time photo of the same woman on a wall of the home, was Libbie Custer.

The experience, which he shared with his teacher, unnerved the educator and haunted Marx for years afterward. He said he's always been prone to experiencing paranormal activity; it is something that has followed him throughout his life. But even at the tender age of twelve, after seeing Libbie's ghost, he knew what he had to do: he had to learn, at least for a while, how to distance himself from the unseen world that seemed to keep reaching out to him. "You open yourself up and stuff follows you," he said. It took time, but he had to learn to shut himself off to the world beyond.

Now, he investigates the paranormal and unexplained.

Marx says there is more than Libbie Custer's ghost that haunts the premises of Fort Abraham Lincoln. He calls the Custer home a "house that is full" of spirits, both intelligent and residual, both human and animal (including the residual haunting of a dog that barks in the basement). And maybe something else. "And it's not just the house—that whole fort is full [of spirits]," he said. "You've got Libbie, who is definitely an intelligent spirit, whom, I'm guessing when she died, migrated back to the place she last saw her husband before he went off to his death." This could be the case even though the house is a replica of her former home and not the actual house itself, he said.

The spirits that linger at the historical property are not only those who have ties to the old fort, but also those who lived here long before the white man arrived. "That entire ground is very active. . . . It's one big piece of ground that is split up into three separate time periods," he said—On-a-Slant Village, Fort McKeen, and Fort Abraham Lincoln, noting the centuries-old history of the site attracts their ghosts.

Marx said the site is full of interesting history, both natural and of the paranormal kind, and noted that the only place on the grounds that, in his estimation, might not be haunted is the old commissary.

It has been said that there cannot be ghosts without history. Those looking for the latter will surely find it at Fort Abraham Lincoln and the Custer House; and they may just encounter some of the former, too.

While here, enjoy the nearby trails and campgrounds. The site also has two seasonal camping cabins, the Goodboy and Sheheke, in the main campground.

THE SPECTER OF LADY BLACK TONGUE

FORT YATES

Fort Yates, located in Sioux County, the tribal headquarters of the Standing Rock Sioux tribe, also has a couple of creepy stories. One may be truer than the other, but both are part of the legend that exists in the small community.

A woman named Lady Black Tongue, according to the legend, used to live on a hill in the vicinity and was hit by a car while walking home on a dark night years ago. Apparently, the woman wasn't your average neighborhood missus. Some say the name "Black Tongue" was not a derogatory or sinister term, or even a medical one referring to oral hygiene (as is a true meaning of the term) but, rather, an honorary or respectful title.

The stories say that Old Lady Black Tongue appears from time to time, dressed in her melancholy garb of black, to unsuspecting travelers that she tries to stop on the roadway in search of the driver who hit her all those many years ago. From the story, it appears she wants revenge. Or is it to make peace with the driver, to perhaps offer forgiveness?

Who's to say, especially since this story sounds like an urban legend rather than a true paranormal occurrence. Either way, the tale remains an interesting one to tell around the campfire or on wind-chilled evenings. Perhaps the best way to find out if the story has any merit is to drive the road to see if Lady Black Tongue appears, trying to hitch a ride or in other ways stop your vehicle.

The other story about Fort Yates has to do with the former Luger Hotel and a little girl who is said to have died there—and often would make her presence known. Guests reported seeing a young girl dressed in white in one of the facility's rooms. It is claimed that some people who slept in room number 4 said the young girl seemingly believed she belonged there, for her visage appeared at the foot of the bed—standing, not saying anything, only making her presence known.

Her young childlike laugh was also heard echoing in parts of the hotel.

Throughout the ages, ever since individuals have reported interactions with the paranormal world, there have been accounts of ghostly young children appearing to their unsuspecting witnesses. Sometimes the child apparition, like the one mentioned above, appears without saying anything. Often a child's phantom laughter is heard. Other times, the alleged spirit child acts mischievous, going so far as to play pranks or jokes on their victims.

Not everyone who believes in ghosts, however, believes a child's spirit truly makes its presence known in such ways. Some people believe it is a false or sinister spirit that appears in child form to deceive the witness.

As with anything having to do with the paranormal, there are suppositions and conjecture galore, without much scientific proof to say definitively what an apparition is, besides the tried-and-true theories of it being a ghost, a wandering spirit, a lost soul.

Or a residual haunting from the past.

What do you believe?

EASTERN
NORTH DAKOTA

BIGFOOT COMES TO NORTH DAKOTA

ELLENDALE

Bigfoot sure gets around.

Stories about Bigfoot, a primate-like creature that stalks North America's forests, have circulated for decades. In 1810, David Thompson, a surveyor and trader, claimed to have seen overlarge footprints near the Columbia River Gorge. They resembled human footprints, he said, only much larger. It wasn't for another 120 years, however, that Bigfoot became legendary in American culture. Originally, most of the alleged sightings occurred in the northeastern part of the country, in places like Pennsylvania, and in the Midwest, such as in Iowa, but eventually sightings began to be reported in California, Oregon, and Washington.

Since then, the mysterious bipedal creature with enormous feet has reportedly been seen from California's redwoods to the Florida Everglades, from Maine's rocky coast to Washington State's rainforests, in the Rocky Mountains and across the country's Great Plains—including North Dakota.

Whence it came, no one knows, but there have been sightings reported across the land.

Yes, Bigfoot sure gets around.

Still, some people find it difficult to believe in such a creature. Even some who believe in the paranormal do not believe the story of Bigfoot.

Those who claim eyewitness accounts tell a different story. The creature really does exist, they say. Some, such as Idaho resident Carol Sherman, have smelled its foul odor and sensed its eerie presence.

Sherman told me, when we met in 2012 as I worked on another book, that she encountered the Bigfoot creature while searching for beaver ponds with her grandson at a location in the South Hills of south-central Idaho. She described it as having a foul scent, resembling a man covered in gray hair, and with yellow eyes. The woods went quiet.

"I noticed right away that something eerie was going on," Sherman said. "I just had this feeling. . . . We noticed it was completely quiet. No birds were singing, nothing; and that wasn't normal." Before long, she heard mumbling, then smelled the foul air, and then heard noises like sticks being banged against each other. Then she saw the frightful visage, a gray figure hunched down. It stood. She turned away, frightened. Sherman and her grandson started walking back to their vehicle and the creature, whatever it was, started following them in the thicket of trees. They soon lost sight of it though, and upon returning to Sherman's truck they drove away.

Once at home, Sherman began to tell people about their encounter, but she felt reprimanded. People told her there was a logical explanation for what they saw; they either imagined the experience or took out of context what they had seen. She looked up the Bigfoot Field Researchers Organization and posted her story on its website. Before long, a researcher from the organization contacted her. She took him to the place of the sighting, a place called Wahlstrom Hollow near Kimberly, Idaho, and the researcher, noticing how branches were broken, said it looked as if several of the creatures were in the area. Sherman thought that sounded right. The mumbling she had heard "didn't sound like just one, but two or three," she said.

Sherman was adamant. There was no smirk or gentle persuasion with the story she told. She shared it bluntly, frighteningly even, describing in detail what she and her grandson had experienced that strange day in Idaho's backcountry.

The reason I share this Idaho tale here is because those who claim to have seen Bigfoot share many similar details. A man, for example, who claimed to have tracked Bigfoot in late 2016 in Ellendale, North Dakota, described the creature as a big, frightening monster in line with the Bigfoot character as Sherman described it.

Ellendale resident and experienced tracker Christopher Bauer told WDAY News in a report dated January 10, 2017, that on Christmas Day he had tracked a Bigfoot for several miles until he lost the creature in the hills. The footprints, he said, were eighteen by eight inches, with a four-foot stance, and left deep impressions in the frozen earth.

Bauer got confirmation of the alleged Bigfoot when a family friend said she spotted the creature through her kitchen window. The hairy bipedal was on a nearby trail, heading across a highway and into the hills. The friend described the creature she had seen as being a "huge, hairy, ugly monster."

Bauer told the news station that while some people may claim it was a hoax perpetrated by someone else to fool him, the footprints were too real to be anything but the real deal. "It's a bigfoot, sasquatch, gigantopithecus, whatever you want to call him," he said. "He's a real animal, he's here and I want people to know."

The topic of the sighting and tracking was brought up again in another WDAY report a couple of weeks later, when it was claimed that a mysterious letter arrived at the station claiming the footprints were meant not as a hoax but a prank. "The letter details how the writer allegedly went for a booze-fueled stroll on a pair of homemade Sasquatch slippers," according to the January 31, 2017, report. It refutes Bauer's claims, but he refuses to budge on his stance about the undiscovered ape. "'This is a real, real animal,' said Bauer."

He called the letter a hoax and the tracks real, claiming the four-foot-wide strides of the prints he found and the alleged fake tracks' lack of heel impressions were on his side of the argument.

At least one large animal expert the news station spoke to wasn't so sure, telling the reporter that large mammals grow thick coats during the cold months and often eat dozens of pounds of food every day. In winter their food supply might be scarce, so they may more readily be seen in more populated areas. "Not exactly a vote of confidence for a giant ape," the report surmised. But Bauer stood by his claim that it wasn't a four-legged creature he had tracked.

The alleged sighting is not the first time a Bigfoot sighting has been reported in the Peace Garden State. In 2004, several people in New Town and Mandaree, on the Fort Berthold Indian Reservation, claimed to have seen a Bigfoot-like creature. Paul Danks, natural resources administrator for the Three Affiliated Tribes, told the *Aberdeen American News* that he had marked the locations of reported sightings on an office map. "People south of New Town said they'd seen basically, I guess . . . Bigfoot," Danks was quoted in the paper. The news report continued: "Tribal officials said they took pictures of tracks, but found nothing conclusive. It is not the first reported sighting of a mysterious big creature in North Dakota. In 1962, a hunter reported that he was stalked by a great ape just outside a mobile home park in Minot."

THE RESIDUAL PRAIRIE BATTLE OF 1862

FORT ABERCROMBIE, ABERCROMBIE

If the Earth and its historic sites, natural and man-made, could speak, what would they tell us? Some believe they do communicate. Often it is through their ghosts.

Fort Abercrombie, located in Abercrombie about thirty-five miles south of Fargo along County Highway 22, has many tales of history to tell and a few ghost stories, too. The stories start with the fort's founding in the mid-1800s.

The fort was established under the direction of Lt. Colonel John J. Abercrombie of the Second US Infantry, for whom it received its name, on August 28, 1858, but two years later was reestablished farther north at its present location due to flooding of the murky river during the spring thaw. It was the first military fort, approved by Congress, to be established in what later became North Dakota. It fulfilled its original purpose—to protect settlers from the Sioux—but later served as the hub for a number of transportation routes through the northern plains, giving it its moniker as the "Gateway to the Dakotas."

According to the State Historical Society of North Dakota, the fort, manned at one time by volunteer soldiers from Minnesota during the Civil War, guarded trails that were used by pioneers, fur traders, and military personnel, as well as the steamboats that would make their way on the Red River. It also served as a supply base for two major gold-seeking expeditions.

The fort proved its mettle even without palisades during a six-week war in 1862 between the United States and Dakota warriors, the latter who had attacked the compound. One of the ghost stories associated with the fort gives a nod to this long-ago conflict on the prairie.

Blockhouses and palisades, which had not been built before the war with the Dakota, were constructed not long afterward, but they were not to remain. The fort was abandoned in 1877, the buildings sold and removed—at least temporarily. By 1939, a reconstruction project by the Works Progress Administration constructed "three blockhouses and stockade. It also returned the military guardhouse to the fort's property."

Today, Fort Abercrombie remains a pillar to the past, where visitors are welcome to learn about the fort's history and catch a glimpse of what life was like at the time. Those with an interest in the paranormal should keep their eyes and ears open for another type of history lesson.

One of the stories associated with Fort Abercrombie is that spirits—some dressed in uniform, others in the dress of the Sioux warrior—have been seen and heard at the site. Apparently, these unembodied spirits of both soldiers and Native Americans, with their spectral weapons of war, reenact, in a residual haunting, the real-life scenes when their armaments clashed on the prairie in the 1860s.

Though this might sound like nothing more than an urban legend meant to spark a different kind of interest in the fort—Utah, for instance, has a similar story of a historic marker—there are other claims of paranormal activity at the century-old site.

People have claimed to have heard chilling screams inside the tower houses. Don't let the ghost stories keep you away.

The Fort Abercrombie grounds are open all year, and visitors can self-guide with the outdoor interpretive signs. The building, however, is open during the day from May 29 to September 6, and by appointment-only from September 6 through October 31. Respect the grounds, enjoy your visit, and do keep an eye and ear peeled for those ghostly battles and sounds. Those whoops and clinking and firing of arms might not be from this world but, rather, something from the historical and otherwise unseen past.

GHOSTLY GRAVES

RIVERSIDE CEMETERY, FARGO

"They're coming to get you, Barbara," the brother says to his sister, his voice sounding full of drool, menacing. Off in the distance, in the background of the graveyard scene, a figure saunters toward the siblings who have come to pay respects to their father, whose body lies beneath one of the headstones. The recessed figure, lumbering among the trees, comes closer and reaches for the girl. The brother fights him off.

Sound familiar? It's the opening scene in the 1968 classic horror film *Night of the Living Dead*, perhaps cementing for all time the notion that cemeteries are places where ghouls and ghosts may wander from their graves.

Beyond George A. Romero's atmospheric black-and-white film—which has also been adapted to a color version—and whatever else Hollywood may depict about cemeteries, human or pet, they can be disturbing for people with wild imaginations or those with sensitive spirits. Their own spirits may tap into the unseen, giving good reason as to why such a place may be spooky.

While there have been no zombie sightings reported at Fargo's largest place of interment, Riverside Cemetery, located at 2102 5th Street South, there has been a number of stories about paranormal occurrences at the hallowed site. Established in 1879, with a burial that took place the year before, Riverside Cemetery is the final resting place for the bodies of some 18,000 individuals.

The United States didn't have any managed cemeteries before 1831, according to Keith Eggener, associate professor of American art and architecture at the University of Missouri. In a March 16, 2011, article by Rebecca Greenfield in *The Atlantic*, Eggener said folks buried their dead back then, of course, but they didn't have the spacious, modern graveyards that exist today. That is a more modern trend that started when Mount Auburn Cemetery in Cambridge, Massachusetts, was established.

Riverside's first burial, which took place before the actual surveying of the land, was that of a woman named Climena Lowell in 1878. Her headstone, a tall, pillar-like structure, tells visitors that she was born on April 25, 1813, and died February 16, 1878. Once the land was surveyed, ownership of blocks went to different individuals. Over the years, the cemetery proper continued to expand, and in 1903 a graveyard association was created, which further enhanced the "booming business of death," according to a North Dakota State University article. It wasn't until 1920 that the site's mausoleum was built.

It is here, in the mausoleum, where some of the cemetery's strangest activity has taken place, according to the stories. A number of voice phenomena have been captured at the cemetery by ghost hunters, including at the mausoleum, where it also is rumored that a phantom tapping can be heard, as if someone inside the mausoleum is trying to make contact with the living on the other side of the wall. As the story goes, put a recording device against it and the tapping will be picked up electronically. If you're lucky, you may hear it with your own ears.

A PARK AND ITS HAUNTED CEMETERIES

TROLLWOOD PARK, FARGO

There are no trolls at Trollwood Park, but there very well might be a few ghosts.

Trollwood Park, located at 3664 Elm Street North, Fargo, on the banks of the Red River of the North, doesn't look unnerving. Just the opposite. It is a family-friendly park with many facilities for activities enjoyed by both kids and adults, such as picnic shelters, a playground, and a disc golf course—the latter can be used in warm weather whenever the park isn't flooded.

Of note, when my wife and I visited the park on May 7, 2022, no one could use the disc course then due to flooding. Golf targets peeked up out of the liquid cold, like sentinel guards, waiting for the recession of the waters. But when the waters recede, Trollwood Park, which comprises twenty-eight acres and is managed by the Fargo Park District, is a pleasant place to toss a ball or frisbee or to share some of mom's home-cooked fried chicken in the shade of its thick trees.

The park also has an interesting history—and three cemeteries within its boundaries—that may lend itself to some of the ghost stories and other strange tales associated with it. In one newspaper article, for instance, the park is described as a "haunted playground." Some of the stories indeed seem to be folklore and urban legend, but those shouldn't discount the episodes of unexplained phenomena that have been reported here by real people who claim to have experienced them.

The roots of Trollwood Park stretch back more than a century to 1895 when Cass County built a hospital and asylum, basically a multipurpose institution on eighty acres that also had a nursing home and halfway house for able-bodied inmates. A farm also was established, which the inmates worked, and fifty-three additional acres were added to the farm in 1916. The hospital operated until 1947, when it was turned into a senior care center until 1973, after which the Fargo Park District took over the property. In 1978, the Trollwood Performing Arts School was established on-site at the former hospital.

Something that speaks volumes about how economically disadvantaged some of the patients and residents—the "low-income patients or the residential paupers"—who died at the old hospital and asylum were is that they were buried on the property. "The county paid for burials in what was named 'Potter's Grave.' The graves were poorly done and did little to recognize who was in the grave," reported an October 31, 2016, article in the *Fargo Forum*.

Interestingly, at least three cemeteries have been located within the park, each marked to alert visitors whether it's cemetery number 1, 2, or 3. According to Carolyn Boutain, enterprise director for the Fargo Park District, "cemeteries at the park is not as odd as people might at first think. That is normal in our industry. . . . They become absorbed into the county park system or into the city park system." Boutain continued to explain that the oldest of the three cemeteries has bodies that were interred around the time of the 1914 influenza outbreak. "The majority of those have not been exhumed," she said, but noted that some bones, both human and animal, have been exposed over the years due to the erosion of that section of the river bank. "There's another cemetery that was put in around the 1930s, I think, and that one is on the northern point and gets flooded quite often. But as far as I understand, all of those bodies are still there. . . . There are no grave markers or anything like that, where you could say, 'Oh, there's so and so.' They're marked by rocks, large boulders on the corners."

The third cemetery, located closest to Broadway on the west side of the park, is the one most recently exhumed. Boutain explained, "The reason those bodies were exhumed is because of flooding, again, the slippage that happened on this side of the hill. People would literally find parts of coffins, rings, pieces of clothing, bone fragments. Those were the most recently buried." She said some bones that have been found at the park likely are that of animals, since the site also was a working farm. "There were horses and pigs and other animals that had been in the facilities there," she said, noting some of the bones found were too big to be human.

Perhaps it is the cemeteries and the bones that have been found here that sparked the ghost stories, though some of the stories stretch back many years. Boutain said one story she's heard is that the lights of the building, when it was used as an arts center, would turn on when no one was inside to flip the switch.

Vicki Chepulis, co-founder of the Trollwood Performing Arts School, which has since moved across the border to Moorhead, Minnesota, said in all the time she spent at the facility when it operated at the park site, she had never experienced anything threatening from the unseen world. There were, however, a number of instances of things happening that she could never explain: a fire that broke out and was mysteriously extinguished; a white dove that would show up every night on the outdoor stage during the performance of *Joseph and the Amazing Technicolor Dreamcoat*; and during the performance of the musical *Oklahoma!* when the cast sang one song that seemed to always attract the same hawk that would fly overhead.

Paranormal? Probably not. But they lend themselves to part of the mystery that seems to be an essence at Trollwood.

Chepulis, who spoke to me by telephone on the morning of May 21, 2022, said she was then living in Minnesota, and hadn't been to Trollwood Park for several years. But it was after she left that she started hearing the ghost stories attached to it. One of those stories, which has all the hallmarks of an urban legend, is about the spirit of a woman who had been seen under one of the site's thick trees, dancing to music as performances took place at the arts center during its heyday at the park. Chepulis never mentioned this story, but it is one that has circulated on some internet sites. Another is of a ghost lady who dances beneath a willow tree while an old farmer, apparently also an apparition, tills the ground. Perhaps the same alleged ghost?

According to a 2016 article by the *Fargo Forum*, a paranormal group visited the park in 2012 and "reportedly confirmed the existence of paranormal entities." The group said that, in one recording, a voice is heard saying "Get out"—a common term phrased by allegedly perturbed spirits at haunted locales. Other stories of the park are about people feeling touched by unseen hands, and some have claimed they felt as if they were being followed by phantom presences.

Whether true or not, Dave Leker, executive director of parks for the Fargo Park District, gave good insight to the park's lore in a 2012 article by the same newspaper. He said if nothing else, "Trollwood's history at least lends itself to the possibility of paranormal activity."

LIGHTS IN THE SKY, BOTH NATURAL AND UNEXPLAINED

FARGO

In the autumn of 2021, while the coronavirus was still raging with a new variant, some people turned their gaze heavenward—not only in prayer but in wonder at a spectacular, natural phenomenon that is witnessed in the northern climes.

Regional newspapers shared images that residents had captured of the Northern Lights. Some television news stations did the same thing. It was impressive to see the many images that people had captured of the phenomenon that turns dark skies green—or pink or blue—but more engaging was seeing the Lights in person. This was not the first time that images of the Northern Lights, taken by residents, were shared by the news media. The Lights come out of their funk every year, bedazzling those lucky enough to witness them.

Atmospheric conditions have to be right, as does the setting, in order to view this spectacular heavenly display. In North Dakota, the Lights are best seen in the darkness of night, away from light pollution. Many online calendars, such as the one maintained by the North Dakota Department of Tourism, hint at the best times to see the Lights. When that happens, find a secluded place, make sure you have your camera at the ready, and turn your gaze heavenward, Let the show begin!

Sometimes, there are other light shows that take place in the skies over North Dakota.

All it takes is a cursory glance at the State Report Index for North Dakota on the National UFO Reporting Center website to see the many eyewitness accounts of strange lights and other activity that has been reported in the skies over the Peace Garden State. While there are not as many reports of UFO sightings here as there are in other states (North Dakota had 192 historic UFO sightings and was ranked number two in states with the fewest recorded sightings, according to a December 21, 2021, posting by Stacker), some of its documented sightings are most remarkable, including an encounter in 1948 that has come to be known as the "Gorman Dogfight" over Fargo.

Like the reports about Northern Lights, news media often publish or broadcast reports about unexplained sightings in the sky. The Gorman Dogfight, one of the more spectacular UFO sightings, has received a lot of media attention over the years, including a December 20, 2020, article by the *Fargo Forum*, which revisited the story more than a half-century after the encounter was first reported.

World War II fighter pilot George F. Gorman was in the cockpit of his P-51 Mustang, flying alongside other pilots on the evening of October 1, 1948, logging flight time. After about thirty minutes, the other pilots he was with decided to head back to base, but Gorman said he wanted more time in the air.

According to a *Fargo Forum* article that ran a few days later, on October 3, Gorman was flying near Hector Field when an air traffic controller told him about a small Piper Cub in the area. Gorman said he saw the plane, but also acknowledged he saw an unidentified aircraft—a disk-like object illuminated by a number of lights. Interested in what the flying object could be, Gorman tried to make contact with it and pursued the craft for nearly a half hour, but the strange craft and whatever was flying it never responded. He said the closer he got to it, the brighter it appeared. After nearly another half hour of pursuing the unidentified object, eventually the much faster UFO soon outpaced him until Gorman lost sight of it.

But not for long. He had apparently caught the interest of whatever was flying the object; it changed course and flew toward him. "When the object was coming head on, I held my plane pointed right at it," Gorman said. "The object came so close that I involuntarily ducked my head because I thought a crash was inevitable. But the object zoomed over my head."

According to the 2020 article, Gorman submitted a sworn statement that he believed there was "definitive thought" behind the maneuvers of the strange craft, as if something intelligent were flying it. He also said it could go much faster than his plane could and maneuver in ways that his craft could not. "Despite what seems to be evidence to the contrary, the Air Force concluded the object was a combination of looking at the planet Jupiter and a weather balloon." Gorman, however, insisted it was not a weather balloon, but he stayed quiet about the incident after being told by the Air Material Command to not divulge further information or face a court-martial if he did.

Gorman's story, which came from a respected fighter pilot, was confirmed by another pilot who was flying that night and by two air traffic controllers. Apparently, Gorman, who was used to chasing enemy aircraft, now could add chasing possible alien spaceship to his record.

HAUNTS, REAL AND OTHERWISE

GRAND FORKS

The year 1997 was like no other for the border communities of Grand Forks, North Dakota, and East Grand Forks, Minnesota. The population at the time was roughly forty-nine thousand, but for a period of time early that year it dwindled significantly. That's because much of the community was evacuated due to widespread flooding.

The two communities—but mostly the North Dakota side—were literally inundated with rising waters from the Red River of the North, a north-flowing river that runs some 550 miles from Breckenridge, Minnesota, to Winnipeg, Canada. Heavy snow that winter, and a saturated basin, caused water to heave beyond its bounds and flood the streets, business districts, and neighborhoods of these "twin cities."

Today, in place of the flood, businesses and homes have been rebuilt and there is a well-developed twenty-mile-plus trail system with pleasant parks that stretch throughout the communities.

But even so, there are ghosts that remain—not so much of the paranormal variety as of memories past, of homes that once were and the lives that had been affected by their loss. Even in the pleasantness of this resilient community today, there is an underlayer of frightening awe, knowing how Mother Nature can turn against an active and robust community and bring it to its knees.

The flood of 1997 made headlines across the globe, and the local paper, the *Grand Forks Herald* and its team of reporters, received a Pulitzer Prize for their reporting of the flood and its aftermath. They never missed a deadline and the daily paper, though printed elsewhere for a time, was published on time every day. Yes, the community of Grand Forks survived the flood, despite the chaos it caused, and it is a stronger, more planned city because of Mother Nature's fit.

And here, also in this welcoming community, there may very well be a few places that have the paranormal kinds of ghosts attached to them as well. Alexander "Blue" Weber, president and CEO of the Downtown Development Association (DDA), seems to think so.

Weber spends a lot of time thinking about his community, particularly the downtown area. By the time we had our first conversation on Friday, July 8, 2022, he had been president for about four years and a member of the Grand Forks community for fourteen. Originally from Utah, he said Grand Forks has been a blessing in his life—a community in which he is fully invested.

The DDA's mission is to advocate, promote, grow, and improve the downtown community. It does so by hosting events, working with developers, and providing bicycles for rent in the downtown area. "Our organization does a lot of things, from working with small businesses to putting on street fairs to being bike mechanics," Weber said, noting that the downtown setting is perfect for him. It's where he worked for a number of years, before his current job running businesses, managing events, and the like. "Urban cores and urban settings are just my favorite," he said. "It is good use of property tax, it is good use of pedestrianism, and it's a high density of local businesses—and so all of the things that are my favorite I get to do on a daily basis."

While the organization contributes to the community by strengthening partnerships, it also creates ways for newcomers and old-timers to learn about the city's historic past such as monthly walking history tours throughout the summer, hosted by Weber and his team partner, Corey Mock.

My wife and I joined Blue on a walking tour on July 9, after our initial phone conversation the day before. It was a Saturday, and the community's farmers market, held at the town square, was just winding down for the day. We met up with Weber and a few other couples, then headed off on the tour.

Our first stop was at the flood marker on the banks of the Red River of the North near the Sorlie Bridge, one of three bridges in the area that connects the two communities. After Weber gave a descriptive history about the flood and its aftermath, and stories about the community's resiliency and determination to not be intimidated by Mother Nature, we headed along the pleasant pathway that runs near the river toward our destination with the buildings downtown.

Weber said there are two routes, which he and Mock alternate every month.

Some businesses that once stood are no longer in town; others look much different than they did before the flood due to new construction to repair damage. Still, others were left much like they have appeared since the city's earliest days.

One of the buildings on the tour was the Herald Building—home of the *Grand Forks Herald*—which, during the flood, was partially destroyed by flood and fire. Later, a portion of the facility was reconstructed. In a fitting tribute to the historic flood, the Herald Building, which today is owned by the city and serves as a tech hub for innovators and entrepreneurs, has a clock tower and many symbols incorporated into the building, giving a nod to the flood of 1997.

As we continued the tour along the Red River, garnering historic episodes from the rail line and the old buildings, there was a sense of the ghosts that linger here in this community—ghost of memories past, of what once had been—and Weber gave brief, interesting tidbits about a number of them, including an old theater and some of the hotels in the area.

Come October, the stories about these buildings turn a bit ghostly. Some of the stories recounted are those that have to do with the Empire Arts Center, which was built in the early days of the last century and is rumored to be haunted by a spirit named "Lester," and of the Antler Hotel where the spirit of the proprietor may still visit.

Weber said many of the ghost stories he garners about the buildings come from talking with the owners or those who work in them: "Everybody kind of has their own versions of scary stories of the old theater." Weber's favorite story to tell: "Probably the one about the Antler Hotel," he said. "I just think that one is a fascinating story." At one point it was called the Frederick Hotel, located at the intersection of 1st Avenue and North 3rd Street. That's where the owner of the hotel, John J. Freeman, was working on an elevator. "I think this was like 1905," Weber said. "He was working on the elevator and somebody pressed the button and it went up and crushed him on the top of the elevator, and then it dropped all the way to the bottom."

And then there is this story: "There are two old hotels that are kitty-corner from each other," Weber said, noting that one of them, the Ryan Hotel, is where the DDA office is located today. It sits kitty-corner to the former Dakota Hotel. "They've had a huge rivalry, like since the beginning of time," he told us. "They've always had a rivalry." The Dakota Hotel burned down multiple times, and the last time was perhaps the most unpleasant of all. A World War I veteran was staying in the hotel with his wife when it caught fire, Weber explained. The woman, for some reason, couldn't wake up her husband but wouldn't leave him as the flames rose. She instead went to the window to call for help to the people on the streets. Could somebody help them?

"She was in the hotel room with her husband as he was burning to death," Weber said. "Both of them did not survive the fire."

A sad outcome, indeed.

"But the thing that makes that whole story fascinating to me is that the Ryan Hotel [now used as low-income housing] has these urns on top," he continued, noting there are thirteen total along 1st Avenue and North 3rd Street. "One of the things done to market the Ryan Hotel was it said, 'Our hotel is so much safer than the Dakota Hotel, for even the Dakota Hotel keeps the ashes of their victims in our building.' . . . It's kind of a sad thing to say, but also funny to think that at one point that's what marketing was for these two hotels."

Weber said Halloween month is a fun time for him to host the tour, because he gets to share some of the stories that otherwise are not told the rest of the year. "We're never making up stories," Weber said, but also noted that he does put the question in people's mind: With what has happened here (name a place), could it be haunted? He explained, for instance, "we tell the story of how he, the hotel proprietor, was there, and we'll say, like, is he still there walking the grounds to this day? Those types of things, because it's more fun during Halloween tours."

Stories such as these also lend themselves to ghost tales, which can serve as another marketing effort, especially during the Halloween season. But with every ghost story, there is history behind it. And that, to Weber, is what makes these tales so interesting. There is much in the way of fascinating history in downtown Grand Forks—and one cannot tell a proper ghost story without historic background.

Take the walking tour, held on the second Saturday of each month during the summer and fall, and learn for yourself. Maybe you'll garner your own experience with the unexplained. If nothing else, you'll be led to believe that there is a real possibility that some of these old buildings might very well house unseen tenants from decades past. As Weber put it, "With so many beautiful historic buildings downtown, it's pretty easy to stand outside of them in October and get creepy vibes from these beautiful old historic buildings that have balconies and things."

THE DEVILS LAKE MONSTER

DEVILS LAKE, GRAND FORKS REGION

What is more believable, ghosts and hauntings, alien spacecraft in the night skies, or strange creatures, such as Bigfoot and lake serpents, that lurk in our natural world?

The answer, of course, varies from person to person. Those inclined to look beyond the mortal sphere of what we definitely know say such things are as natural to this globe as are sunflowers on Dakota farmland. Others, even some who believe in the paranormal, have a tough time accepting the notion that bipedal primates stalk the backcountry across North America, or that a prehistoric serpent haunts a highland lake in Scotland. Such beliefs go too far off-kilter. The paranormal is real, they say, but alien craft and unknown monsters, no way. And then there are the full-fledged skeptics, of course, who say all of the above, including ghosts, are nothing but fairy tales created by overactive imaginations. Lastly, some people, having no proof one way or the other, accept at least the possibility of such unnatural strangeness in our natural world.

As with ghost stories, when it comes to tales of strange creature sightings, it seems that every state has them. The stories usually have roots from long ago. Case in point: an alligator-like monster has been reported to haunt the chilly depths of a popular lake in the Grand Forks region of North Dakota, between Grand Forks and Minot. This creature is known as "the Devils Lake Monster."

Contemporary stories about the Devils Lake Monster have circulated since about 1894 when the *New York Sun* published an article on October 21 alleging that the "serpent" had "alligator jaws and glaring red eyes" and a tail that was "about 80 feet long."

In further description of the monster, the article described it thus:

The serpent usually appears in August and about sunset. The red glare of the sunset sky is often reflected in the eyes of the serpent like mirrors and the flashes of red light that go darting here and there as the serpent turns its head strike terror into the hearts of those on whom they fall. The serpent moves slowly along about a half mile from the shore, and in the course of a day or two makes the round of the lake. At times it lashes the water furiously with its tail and it leaves a simple shining wake as it pushes its way along.

More than twenty years later, stories of the alleged monster were still being told. An article in a newspaper closer to home, the *Grand Forks Daily Herald* (now the *Grand Forks Herald*), published a story on July 21, 1915, describing how the monster had been seen floating in the water, apparently unmindful or uncaring of the crowds that watched from shore. With the jarring headline, "That Devils Lake Sea Serpent Basks in Sunshine for Admiring Crowds; Now They'll Hunt It," the story, in part, reads:

Stretched out on the surface of the bay of Devils Lake, fronting Chautauqua, the monster sea serpent basked. In the delightful evening sunshine shortly before sundown last night, while residents of Chautauqua and Greenwood looked on in silent amazement. The serpent was viewed from several different points.

There was no mistake about it. The monster, that has figured in the legends of Devils Lake for half a century, when only the Indians inhabited the country, or a descendant which answers the earliest description, was seen by so many that no one disputes the fact that it lives in the waters of the lake.

Anglers, businessmen, church pastors, policemen, and leisure lizards all reported seeing the strange water creature that appeared unlike any other type of animal they had seen before. It was also reportedly seen a quarter-mile from shore, in the far east end of the lake, and in its western portions, and was described this time as "between fifty and sixty feet long and between a foot and two feet in diameter."

Stories of the alleged Devils Lake Monster, apparently, have been around longer than the more contemporary and sensationalized newspaper accounts. The stories were part of Native American lore for a long time. One can only imagine how the tales may have both thrilled and chilled youngsters. Perhaps parents used the legend as a fable to teach their children to stay close to shore and not venture into the lake unattended.

The reporter of the *Herald* article noted that, while the story of the lake monster is a good tale to tell around a campfire, no photos exist of the creature and that reports of its sighting had died down over the years, "perhaps due to the seeming scientific impossibility of the creature." He also brought up another interesting point: Devils Lake has no natural outlet, and while the tribes said the monster became stranded "after the last glaciers retreated, that would necessitate a lifespan of 9,000 years or more for the beast." Why, with all of the technology we have today, from satellites in space to the smartphones in our pockets, has there not been any hard proof of the alleged lake monster?

Why, indeed—the same with Bigfoot and Scotland's legendary Loch Ness Monster?

Before writing off the Devils Lake Monster, however, it must be remembered that most folk legends have some basis in fact. What are the facts related to this alligator-like monster that allegedly haunts—or at least at one time haunted—this cold lake in North Dakota? And why has there been a number of witnesses over the years who claim to have seen the strange creature?

Could it be that there really was a strange creature? Or was it not a monster at all but, rather, some deformed or unknown species that had been unexpectedly seen by bystanders?

What is the fact behind the monster legend? It has been a while since the monster has been seen in the murky depths of Devils Lake, but every so often a newspaper article and other stories pop up about it, reviving the legend.

There is one explanation as to why the creature has been so elusive: the unexplained, including strange creatures, are meant to be elusive and kept unexplained, adding to the mystery of life and our own existence on this strange, hospitable planet.

SOUTH DAKOTA is best known for Mount Rushmore, that iconic mountain in the Black Hills where the faces of four of the country's presidents are carved: George Washington, Thomas Jefferson, Abraham Lincoln, and Theodore Roosevelt. The famous mountain (those who live in the shadow of the Rockies say it is only a hill) attracts more than two million visitors every year; and while it indeed is an artistic spectacle, there is much more to this beautiful state than the sculptured mountain.

The Black Hills and Badlands were home to Indigenous tribes long before the white man arrived, and one monument that depicts this heritage is Crazy Horse Memorial—the Lakota's own version of Mount Rushmore. Also, the South Dakota Department of Tourism does a good job of promoting attractions in the state, including its tribal destinations. In June 2022, the department released its "Guide to Tribal Nations: Oceti Sakowin Homelands." Produced and approved through members of the South Dakota Native Tourism Alliance, the guide features a map of tribal lands, brief histories of each tribe, visitor etiquette suggestions, and destinations that provide opportunities to learn more about each tribe.

"Research shows us that our domestic and international visitors are eager to learn more about the culture and history of our friends and partners within South Dakota's tribal nations," James Hagen, the state's secretary of the Department of Tourism, said in a press release announcing the guide, noting that it is an "excellent resource as they plan their experience in our state."

It is refreshing to see something like this—an entire state excited about its Native heritage and going to great lengths to promote it.

In another statement released a few months earlier, in February 2022, forecasting that year's tourism season, Hagen said the state continued to show impressive tourist numbers despite the coronavirus pandemic. "Data shows that travelers have an interest in exploring rural America as they seek outdoor experiences with road trips and visits to national and state parks," he said. "South Dakota offers all of this and more in spades."

As impressive as are the artistic works of Crazy Horse and Rushmore, it is Mother Nature's handiwork that provides endless opportunity in this rugged state—from bubbling springs and rushing rivers to expansive vistas and adventurous trails.

While sharing a partial name with its neighbor to the north, South Dakota is unique among the Dakota states, in that there is more hilly terrain here, more wooded ecosystems. And while both have their Badlands, South Dakota's colorful monuments are topped with jagged peaks.

The Mount Rushmore State shares something else with North Dakota: both joined the Union on November 2, 1889. North Dakota became the thirty-ninth state, South Dakota the fortieth. The reason for this sequence is because that same year a dispute arose about where to place the capital for the Dakota Territory. Resolution came by splitting the territory into North and South, paving the way for each to become its own state. North Dakota was admitted first.

As with any state, South Dakota has had its share of homegrown celebrities, such as George McGovern, Tom Brokaw, Philip Graham, Russell Means, and Cheryl Ladd, among others. Even Laura Ingalls Wilder has some ties to the state.

Among all this history and intrigue—or perhaps entwined with it—are the more unsettling episodes and places. From disembodied spirits and freakish ghouls to the sightings of animated, unexplained objects in the sky to weird creature sightings, South Dakota is a place of mystique and mystery where, sometimes, things really do go bump in the night—and sometimes during the daytime, too.

This land where once dinosaurs tread is a haunted place. As Samuel L. Jackson's character in the movie *Jurassic Park* was wont to say, "Hold on to your butts." Things are about to get weird, as we explore the history, lore, and real-person witness accounts of the ghostly and strange in South Dakota.

WESTERN
SOUTH DAKOTA

CEMETERY SPOOKS IN THE SHADOW OF MOUNT RUSHMORE

MOUNTAIN VIEW CEMETERY, KEYSTONE

It makes sense to start stories of South Dakota history and hauntings with the city of Keystone, population three hundred by 2020 census estimates, where the state's most popular tourist attraction is located—that iconic presidential mountain known as Mount Rushmore National Memorial.

Keystone is one of those places that, if not for its famous mountain, a visitor might blink and miss while driving through. With its small population of residents, it nonetheless feels much larger because of the crowds it attracts most of the year long. During the peak tourist season, when the temperature rises and evenings are pleasant, visitors can purchase a helicopter ride over the valley or eat some of the best pancakes found in the Midwest. And if they're looking for something spooky, they might try visiting the local cemetery, where tales are told about disembodied voices and wandering phantoms.

Some of those interred at the burial grounds are those who worked on Mount Rushmore, a fourteen-year project that started in 1927 when, four years before, Doane Robinson of the South Dakota Historical Society proposed that a monument be built in the granite cliffs of the Black Hills as a way to market the state. Senator Peter Norbeck got behind the idea and helped secure funding for the project. But an artist had yet to be chosen.

Enter Gutzon Borglum, an American sculptor born to Latter-day Saint emigrants in 1867 near Bear Lake on the Utah-Idaho border. Borglum had years earlier set his path on the field of art, and by the time he was commissioned to sculpt Mount Rushmore had already made a name for himself with a number of art projects: Mares of Diomedes, which represents the moment Hercules causes Diomedes's man-eating horses to flee their stable and stampede to the sea, and which is at the Metropolitan Museum of Art in New York City; a large equestrian bronze of General Phil Sheridan that Theodore Roosevelt unveiled in Washington; a memorial to Pickett's Charge on the Gettysburg Battlefield; and the Wars of America memorial and the Seated Lincoln in Newark, New Jersey.

Of all of his creations, however, it is Mount Rushmore that people remember best, even if his name is not widely known as it has been eclipsed by his famous sculpture. Of that monumental piece of art, "Mount Rushmore has grown in fame as a symbol of America—a symbol of freedom and hope for people from all cultures and backgrounds," reads a description by the National Park Service.

But in recent years, there has also been controversy over the monument.

During nationwide protests in 2020, a number of statues and other historic emblems across the country that depicted America's past and its leaders were brought to the forefront of controversy, with some saying the monument should be removed because at least some of the presidents it memorializes were slaveholders. It has also been argued that the national monument itself is on land that is sacred to Native tribes and that, as such, the carving is a desecration. The monument was built on land taken by the white man, the controversy states, land that the Indigenous peoples of the area had enjoyed for centuries. It should be returned to them.

Those on the opposite side of the aisle have defended the memorial—and other emblems across the country—saying they are all part of America's past and that, whether we like it or not, they should remain to teach us of where we have been, how far we have come, and, in essence, not to repeat the same mistakes. They also say these emblems do not honor America's misdeeds but the positive sides of the country. Washington, for instance, may have been a slaveholder but he also did much good for the country as its famous general and first commander in chief.

There is validation for both sides of the argument (though a person may not see the validation of the other side because she or he is so steeped in her or his own values); but no matter where one may stand, one thing we all can agree on is that Mount Rushmore is, for art's sake, an impressive work.

Borglum chose as his centerpiece the four presidents—Washington, Jefferson, Lincoln, and Roosevelt—because he believed they represented different periods of strength of the United States. Washington, as the most prominent figure on the mountain, represents the birth of the United States; Jefferson its growth; Roosevelt its development; and Lincoln its preservation.

Borglum, his vision notwithstanding, wasn't the only artist on the mountain. Some four hundred people worked on the massive sculpture, including his son Lincoln Borglum. What might be little known, especially to first-time visitors to the monument, is that the massive sculpture was not done with only chisel; blasting also was part of the sculpture's creation. "The work was exciting, but dangerous," according to information from the National Park Service, noting that "90% of the mountain was carved using dynamite. The powdermen would cut and set charges of dynamite of specific sizes to remove precise amounts of rock." For their work, sculptors received $8 in pay every day, good money at the time, considering the equivalent was, according to one source, $158.19 in 2022.

Originally, Borglum wanted a written description to accompany the presidential faces, which would describe what he considered the nine most important events in US history, from 1776 to 1906. But the entablature, which was to be fashioned in the shape of the Louisiana Purchase and measuring 80 feet by 120 feet, would not hold text large enough to be read at a distance. Also, Jefferson's head had to be relocated, and that section of the mountain was needed for Lincoln's noggin. The Park Service says a "more lasting plan was developed."

That plan was a seventy-foot tunnel blasted into the mountain between 1938 and 1939, but that work also came to an end when Congress said work should focus on the presidential faces. It wasn't until August 9, 1998, when a repository of records—a teakwood box inside a titanium vault and covered by a granite capstone—was placed in the floor of the cavity's entry hall.

A quote by Borglum on the capstone reads: "Let us place there, carved high, as close to heaven as we can, the words of our leaders, their faces, to show posterity what manner of men they were. Then breathe a prayer that these records will endure until the wind and rain alone shall wear them away."

Borglum never got to see his finished masterpiece. He died on March 6, 1941, just several days before he was to turn seventy-four and not quite eight months before the sculpture was completed. It was finally finished on October 31, 1941—Halloween—with an estimated cost of $989,992.32.

History states that, thankfully, no one was killed during the creation of the iconic faces, but many of the workers, once they passed from this life, were interred at the nearby cemetery. Some of those who were buried at the cemetery are said to have come back from the great beyond to roam their final resting place. It is not uncommon to feel unnerved when visiting a cemetery, but among the reports of strangeness here are phantom figures wandering the premises, ghostly voices and laughter heard when no one else is around, and other oddities such as figures being caught in photos when it was apparent no person was in front of the camera when the picture was taken.

If any place is haunted by the spirits of the dead, it makes sense that a cemetery would be prime real estate. According to the stories, such is the case with

Mountain View Cemetery, which sits in the shadow of Mount Rushmore and has ties to that stately, artistic hill.

UFOS OVER THE NATIONAL MONUMENT

MOUNT RUSHMORE, KEYSTONE

An interesting story related to Mount Rushmore comes from, of all places, Taiwan, though the depicted images to which the story refers are, quite frankly, out of this world.

Scott C. Waring, a UFO enthusiast living in Taiwan, claims to have found an image that he says resembles a "human-like alien species" carved into a mountainside of the Red Planet, much like the faces at Earth's famous presidential mountain in South Dakota. The image that he posted on his blog site on September 22, 2021, and found a home in the tabloid *The Sun* does resemble some sort of face, perhaps the way a viewer with a little imagination can make out pictures in the clouds. Waring, no scientist, writes in his post, which he gave permission for media to use as long as he is properly credited, that "from the wear and tear of the surface, I think that this is over 100,000 years old!" Waring gives his perspective of the find, writing: "This face gives us some idea of what the aliens looked like on Mars long ago. They clearly were intelligent since they carved this face in the side of the mountain. Undeniable proof that intelligent life once roamed the surface of Mars."

This isn't the first time Waring has shared information about what he believes to be faces carved into the hard crust of the Martian planet. He posted in 2015 that a former UN worker, Andre Gignac, claimed to have found evidence through his studies of NASA photos that life, at one time, did exist on Mars. His proof: Gignac claimed to have "identified a bare-breasted female alien, the corpse of another being, a four-legged robot and Mount Rushmore-(style) carvings of historical Martian leaders." Again, there is no scientific proof here, only one ufologist's opinion. The study of photos, for most people, is not a methodology that leads to scientific proof.

As for the legitimate scientists, they have been sending spacecraft to Mars since the 1970s—and, yes, capturing images. In more recent years, NASA has sent five rovers—Sojourner (1997), Spirit and Opportunity (2004), Curiosity (2012), and Perseverance (2021)—to explore the distant globe. While the rovers have discovered some interesting features, including evidence of water, there have been no current life forms detected on the planet that inhabits space some 293 million miles from Earth. Some of the findings are that, like Earth, Mars "has volcanoes, gullies, and flat plains," according to information from NASA. "Scientists can also see channels that look like they were carved by rivers and streams a long, long time ago."

Does this mean life truly did exist on Mars at one time in eons long past? The determination of that, at this point in time, is inconclusive; but it does point to the very real possibility that, yes, some type of life form once inhabited the Red Planet. If so, could Waring's theory be true? Could an alien species somehow impress or engrave its image onto a mountain range? If so, it happened long before Gutzon Borglum took his chisel and dynamite to carve Mount Rushmore's presidential faces, and thus our Martian friends did not get the idea from us earthlings.

But that doesn't mean that creatures from distant galaxies have not watched Earth in more recent times and do not, perhaps, keep watching today. Many UFOs have been reportedly seen in the skies across South Dakota, starting long before modernity to the very present, including some instances of bright lights and fast-moving objects in the Black Hills near Mount Rushmore.

The *Capital Journal* published an article on September 4, 2021, by the South Dakota Historical Foundation that was headlined "Nearly 150 years of Recorded UFO Sightings across South Dakota." In it, the article relates several of the sightings, including one by a woman named Annie Tallent who was part of the Gordon Party in the late 1800s. According to the record, Tallent wrote of her experience during the winter of 1874–1875, explaining:

> About noon, on a clear, cold day, an awful rushing, roaring sound was heard above and to the north of us. It was almost directly over our camp. Everyone immediately looked in that direction and saw an object rushing through the air from east to west, not more than one-half mile above the tree tops, and seemingly not more than three quarter of a mile distant from us.
>
> It seemed almost white and looked at least if it might be 30 or 40 feet in diameter, although its size could not be ascertained with any degree of accuracy. As it seemed surrounded with steam or smoke,

it did not appear to be falling but continued in a horizontal course. Three or four seconds after having passed out of our sight to the west, a report was heard that fairly shook the Hills, while its track clouds of smoke were left that could be seen for 20 minutes after.

Aircraft had not yet been invented when Tallent recorded her account. It was written long before today's technology, at a time when only the horse and wagon were people's primary means of transportation and they had yet to look to the sky to traverse the airy miles.

"It was the grandest sight I had ever witnessed," Tallent said of what she had witnessed that winter day in the Black Hills. Tallent also said—and whether this had anything to do with changes in the season is debatable—that "there was one thing that was very evident, immediately after this sighting, the weather began to grow colder, and continued to increase in intensity each day for about three weeks."

What did Tallent see overhead all those many decades ago?

Today, when an unexplained aerial phenomenon has been witnessed in the sky, there is much debate about what it may have been—a secret government experiment, a weather balloon, et cetera. But what explanations were there during Tallent's day, other than natural phenomena or something from the outer limits of humankind's reach?

Many other unexplained objects have been witnessed in the skies over Mount Rushmore. The South Dakota Historical Society Foundation took note of this, writing in the same *Capital Journal* article: "The National Unidentified Flying Object Reporting Center lists about 350 reported sightings of objects described as resembling dinner plates, orbs, saucers, glowing objects, fireballs, Ferris wheels, globes and more in the skies over the Mount Rushmore state. Most of the listings began in 1947 and continued from there."

TALE OF THE PHANTOM ANGLER

PACTOLA RESERVOIR, PENNINGTON COUNTY

A ghostly fisherman haunts the shores of Pactola Reservoir, a smile on his face as he casts his line. And why shouldn't he be smiling? Because one thing is for sure—this ghost haunts a beautiful location.

Located about eighteen miles west of Rapid City in the Black Hills, the roughly 785-acre reservoir has some fourteen miles of shoreline and water depths of up to 150 feet. It is, according to the US Forest Service, the largest body of water in the Black Hills National Forest.

Could it also be the most haunted?

The reservoir has quite a few inlets, which viewed aerially, make this freshwater fishery look like a wonky jigsaw puzzle. Surrounded by lush forest, the scene is picture-perfect, just right for a postcard or wall calendar. Down below on the shores, people come here from near and far to take in the scenery and to bask in its many offerings, boating and fishing being the most popular. Anglers come here to try their luck with rod and reel, and many have pulled large, record-breaking fish out of its blue-green waters—and not just during summer. This is a popular fishery for ice fishing when Old Man Winter arrives. But some people come here for another activity: scuba diving. (Though, obviously, that's an activity best reserved for the warmer months!)

The reason for the scuba attraction is that here at Pactola, beneath the shimmering waves, is what's left of a town—or at least that's the rumor that seems to attract these underwater gurus with tanks on their backs. What they don't realize until they go underwater, however, is that the stories are fabrications of the truth. According to the South Dakota Department of Tourism, the only visible remnant of the former town is a lone cabin that sits downstream—visibly seen above water.

Another fact: there really was a town named Pactola—and the reservoir is now located where it once stood, a bustling little town in its heyday that eventually dried up as people moved on. As with many towns that came to life in the 1800s, it was the promise of riches that had drawn in its first inhabitants.

First called Camp Crook, named after General George Crook, the town's genesis stretches back to 1875, when Crook and his regiment discovered gold in the area's creek beds. Sneaky miners, those who violated the Treaty of Fort Laramie in hopes of garnering their own treasures from the land, were driven away. They returned the following year when the mills opened and claims along the river began to be filed. The rumor of gold, and the promise of riches, grew and so did the town—a store and post office, among other businesses, opened to serve the growing populace. Soon, a rail line was established as was the Black Hills' first hotel, in 1876, called the Sherman House, named after James Comyon Sherman, an early miner and entrepreneur to the area. The hotel became a stage station along two different stage lines.

But the town wasn't done changing names.

In 1878, it changed to Pactola, named by journalist H. N. Maguire and derived from the Greek placer mining operations of Pactolus River in Lydia, which is now the modern republic of Turkey. The secluded Black Hills town continued to attract people, sometimes not always the best and brightest. Like many gold rush towns, Pactola had its share of shady characters. As such, there arose saloons, gambling halls, and brothels. It was the tracer mines that kept the people here, but as eventually happens with any town that promises riches, the gold dried up and the people left—at least most of them did. Buildings were abandoned.

The town revived over the ensuing decades when "a Civilian Conservation Corps camp, church camps, a facility for tuberculosis patients, lodges, homes, and stores were constructed," according to information in the *Black Hills Visitor Magazine*. "Despite the new buildings, it became largely abandoned due to dwindling mining profits."

By the 1950s it was proposed to build a dam. That project got underway in 1952 and was completed in 1956. During its construction, many of the town's structures—not all of them—were removed from the area and relocated, some to nearby Silver City, before the waters engulfed the town, thus creating Pactola Reservoir.

As for the ghostly angler who appears from time to time, the legend says it has nothing to do with the watery ghost town but instead is caused by a tragic drowning that happened here decades ago. According to Travel South Dakota, the travel and tourism segment of the Mount Rushmore State, the *Rapid City Journal* published a story by Bob Willis in its January 20, 1984, edition that said a man who frequented Rapid Creek with his fishing pole had one day, after allegedly going "mad for reasons unknown," fallen through the ice and drowned. It wasn't until spring that his body was found and laid to rest, but apparently his spirit may have remained.

The tourism department's story on Haunted Outdoors of South Dakota says reports started about people seeing the "mad Pactola fisherman" ("mad," in this instance, perhaps meaning crazy instead of angry). Apparently, he was still casting his line, a smile on his face and doing what he loved in life, searching for his next catch. He seems to not have found a prime fishing hole, however, because he has been seen in several places along Rapid Creek. "He reportedly looked so lifelike that one might not even know he was a ghost," according to the story. "However, if he caught a fish, it mysteriously never had a hook mark in the lip."

Perhaps a man did drown in the river on a cold day in the winter of 1984—I could not verify the report—but the other stories about the ghostly fisherman seem like a tall tale that fishermen tell, especially since another story says the freaky fisherman is trapped under the ice and the cracking heard is not the spring thaw but the mad angler trying to free himself from the cold depths of the lake.

Fable or not, the story of Pactola's phantom fisherman fits well with the other, definitely true stories about the lake—that of it once being a town where the reservoir now lies.

A TOWN FULL OF HISTORY AND HAUNTINGS

DEADWOOD

Kim Ferrel Keehn knows a lot about the ghosts of Deadwood. And why shouldn't she? She retells their stories multiple times a day on her Haunted History Walking Ghost Tour, a business she started in 2019. Before that she served as tour guide at the Bullock Hotel and with Boot Hill Tours. She also has had personal experiences with the paranormal, which makes her tours more realistic because what she teaches on her tours comes from both the heart and lots of personal research. "Being the history geek that I am, and being interested in the paranormal, it was just a perfect marriage," she said of her decision to start the tours. She also learned something about history over the years: "History is not stagnant. It is always changing. I am always researching. New stuff becomes available, and so you never know when you might run across something cool."

She tries to stay clear of folklore and tall tales, telling only the verified history and, as much as possible, verified hauntings of Deadwood in a simple and straightforward fashion: there are indeed things that go bump in the night in this Old West–style town, but the history is as fascinating as any ghost tale. It is the history, in fact, that makes the ghost stories pop. She shares the following quote by paranormal writer Jeff Belanger on her website: "A ghost is history demanding to be remembered."

Keehn's tours keep her busy during the summer months, the height of the tourist season when the 1,500-plus population of Deadwood grows by leaps and bounds with more than two million visitors. She often is on the street, taking guests on one-hour and fifteen-minute tours multiple times a day. She said she has literally worn out the soles of her boots by how much walking she does in a season. But she keeps doing it, not only because the tours are her livelihood but also because she remains fascinated by Deadwood history and the ghosts who seem to remain. It is as if, like in Belanger's quote, they demand that their tales be told. Those tales are indeed found in the history of Deadwood, a town that sprang to life in the late 1800s and that today is proud of its legacy—even if some of its history is less than pleasant. It is, in fact, those unsavory aspects that help bring its ghost stories to life.

Deadwood emerged during the Black Hills Gold Rush of 1876. People came seeking riches, businesses sprang up—saloons and brothels, among them—and the unsavory were drawn to it like old-timers to sarsaparilla. Names most often remembered here are outlaws and madams, local entrepreneurs and developers, and other Old West charismatic characters who came to Deadwood in its earliest days. "Wild Bill" Hickok and Calamity Jane are two of the most popular.

The history here also tells that at least three major fires broke out in town, and Deadwood has experienced a number of economic trials over the decades. If not for legalized gambling that came to Deadwood in 1989, helping the city to thrive, the site might have gone down in history as another ghost town. It survived, thankfully, but it is a ghost town nonetheless, only in a different, more spectral way.

An entire book could be written—and many have been—about Deadwood. Some, such as *Haunted Deadwood: A True Wild West Ghost Town* by Mark Shadley and Josh Wennes, highlight its haunted history. But a person cannot truly grasp the history or the haunts here unless one takes Keehn's haunted walking tour.

The tours start at Saloon No. 10 at 657 Main Street—not the original saloon built in the 1800s, but the present-day saloon built in the 1930s; a place that nonetheless has its share of history and lore. Louie Lalonde, general manager of the establishment, said her father purchased the building in 1963 and it has remained in the family ever since. "We're a bona fide family business, there's no doubt about it," she said.

"Anybody and everybody can work here if they're part of the family and many of them do. . . . Fortunately, my father was a great historian and loved to read and snoop and uncover information and put all the pieces of the puzzle together. He brought a broader meaning to what Saloon No. 10 is today, because he understood how important it was to really continue to tell the story [of Deadwood]. We've tried to live up to one of our slogans, which is the only museum in the world with a bar, and in the summer months we shoot Wild Bill—a staged reenactment of the shooting—four times a day."

Gunslinger James Butler Hickok, or Wild Bill Hickok, was shot in the back of the head by Jack McCall while playing cards at the original saloon on August 2, 1876. The reenactment of the shooting has been going on since the 1980s. That's a lot of times over the years that Wild Bill has relived his final moments, but it is all done for the sake of history. Wild Bill does, however, get a reprieve on Sundays. "We figured we should let him have a day of rest from being shot four times a day during the rest of the week," Lalonde said.

In a thoughtfull discussion about the value of authenticity, Lalonde shared with me how the saloon endeavors to keep history alive:

> You know, so many of those experiences here at Saloon No. 10 are important for people that are coming through. I think one of the bigger parts of the whole experience, for me personally and I know for other family members, is that we have so many people come through that were here years and years ago with their dads and their parents; they remember coming in and maybe sitting at the bar, sitting in one of the barrel chairs, and having a sarsaparilla. Now we see them coming back today and bringing their own children and reliving that experience they had way back with their parents.
>
> I think that in this day and age, more often than not, you see so many businesses trying to adapt to what is important right now. With the gaming in Deadwood, it was probably what everybody needed to do in order to be successful. . . . Everybody thought all they had to do was put in the cool silver money-making machine and all would be well; but there's a lot more to gaming and being successful than just that.

Some places have changed to "look like something out of Las Vegas," Lalonde said. "For some locations that was a good thing. But I think for just the sheer fact that Deadwood is a national historical landmark, those little parts of the history need to be preserved. It's the fabric of who and what Deadwood is and that's what people come to see." Thus, in part, the Wild Bill shooting reenactment that is a popular draw and helps keep history alive amidst the silver slot machines of today. Keehn said she and Wild Bill sit outside the saloon almost every afternoon during their workdays, shooting the bull, waiting for 5 p.m. to arrive. "He has a 5 o'clock show," she said, "and I have a 5 o'clock tour."

Lalonde, who said she chooses not to believe in the paranormal, said there are stories of the unexplained associated with her place of business but declined to share any of them, instead referring me to Keehn. We had already visited, and Keehn, who lived above Saloon No. 10 at one time years ago, said of the establishment that there have been unexplained disturbances at the facility. She personally has experienced some of that, including the phantom smell of women's perfume.

"Upstairs currently is the Deadwood Social Club but there used to be apartments up there," she explained, noting there used to be reports about paranormal activity from tenants and employees. "When I first moved to Deadwood that's where I lived. I had an old Victorian couch that I was going to have recovered because it was full of pinecones. I was pulling the pinecones out one day and I started to smell strong perfume." She had two dogs who "were freaking out." The same thing happened a decade later, when the phantom scent unexpectedly returned.

Many other sites are visited and discussed on the walking tour, but additional businesses did not respond to messages to share their stories. But one is the Bullock Hotel, where Keehn once worked as a tour guide. The Bullock, as well as other establishments in the area, share some of their folk legends on their respective websites.

Keehn said with Deadwood's deep history and the paranormal stories associated with so many places, it is the perfect place to host her tours. Her busy season is from about Memorial Day to Labor Day, but she hosts them all year. Around November, however, when the temps cool, she puts the word out on her website that people will need to give her at least a twenty-four-hour notice that they'd like to take a tour.

Anyone coming to Deadwood to learn about the creepy goings-on in this haunted town—haunted by its literal past as much as the ghosts that may remain—would be well-served by the Haunted History Walking Ghost Tour. Check out the website: hauntedhistorywalkingghosttour.com.

Don't come expecting to experience the paranormal, but know that you very well might.

Keehn—who, beyond continually learning history, continues to learn about the paranormal world—said it best: "I think the thing I have learned is that it is complicated. There is not just one kind of haunting," she said. "There are intelligent hauntings, there are residual hauntings. I don't think you can fit into a box or even explain it all. Like with a residual haunting, it might happen only once a year, on an anniversary or something. A lot of people think . . . it is like in our instant, push-button, search-Google society; they think when they go on a ghost tour that the haunting is actually going to show up on demand. There are no hauntings on demand, but people expect that."

HISTORY AND MYSTERY AT BOOT HILL

MOUNT MORIAH CEMETERY, DEADWOOD

There is a tranquil graveyard in Deadwood where some of the Old West's most famous—and infamous—are interred. It's called Mount Moriah Cemetery, at times dubbed Boot Hill Cemetery, and is located at 1 Mount Moriah Drive. The reason for its popular nickname is because some of the individuals who are buried here are said to have died with their boots on. The nickname, Boot Hill, is not unique to this hallowed spot. It was a popular name for cemeteries that was formed in the 1800s, according to Kevin Kuchenbecker, historic preservation officer with the Deadwood Historic Preservation Office. He also serves as sexton of historic cemeteries—Mount Moriah and two other burial grounds, St. Ambrose Cemetery and Oakridge Cemetery. "Even on our brochure, we call it the Black Hills Boot Hill," he said. "Our first cemetery was established in 1876, the original cemetery, but that was moved up to Mount Moriah in 1878 so we could develop where the original cemetery was; it was on flatter ground."

At Boot Hill, or Mount Moriah, the likes of Wild Bill Hickok and Calamity Jane are interred, as are the bodies of other old-timey gunslingers. There are also many, many more bodies who make this cemetery their final resting place—some 3,600 to be exact—according to Kuchenbecker. He gave a quick overview of some of the names found here:

It is the final resting place of Wild Bill Hickok, Calamity Jane, and Preacher Smith, who was shot August 22, 1876, on his way to provide mass as Crooks City. We still don't know if it was Native Americans or highwaymen who took him. We have Dora DuFran, who was a famous Madame in Deadwood; she's buried with her parrot. Potato Creek Johnny, who found the largest gold nugget in the Black Hills on Potato Creek; it's seven and three-quarter troy ounces and is on display at the Adams Museum. Col. John Lawrence, of Lawrence County where Deadwood is, is buried up there. Seth Bullock, the first sheriff of Deadwood and made famous nationally with the HBO series, is buried (with his wife Martha) above Mount Moriah near an overlook of Mount Roosevelt. He was president of the Black Hills Pioneer Society and personal friend of Theodore Roosevelt. . . . W. E. Adams, an early pioneer and entrepreneur in town. . . . There's a number of Civil War veterans, early historians. We have . . . a Jewish section and a Chinese section—some very early pioneers that made a difference in Deadwood are buried there.

Located above Deadwood Gulch, with distant views of the Homestake Mine and other local haunts, the cemetery was established in 1878 by the Lawrence County Commission. As the preservation office touts on its website, which also includes brochures and maps of the site, the cemetery "is the final resting place of western legends, murderers, madams, and pillars of Deadwood's early economic development." However, Mount Moriah "is more than just a graveyard. It offers visitors an opportunity to enjoy a Late Victorian cemetery set in the backdrop of the northern Black Hills. The paved roads in the cemetery provide an excellent opportunity to explore the site."

And that's what hundreds of thousands of people do every year.

Deadwood, being a national historic site, attracts about two million tourists every year, and of that number some 800,000 to 1,000,000 people visit Mount Moriah Cemetery annually, Kuchenbecker said. People come from across the country and around the globe to experience this rough-and-ready town that came to life in an era when nobody gave two thoughts to a man carrying a holster on his belt, a time when the Black Hills were still being explored by fur trappers and miners. To the tribes, however, this land had already been their home for a long time. But change was in the air.

Once established, Deadwood itself would see itself change over the years. In its earliest days, it didn't always attract the best people. Here came a mix of ambitious entrepreneurs and sketchy gunslingers, where drinking, gambling, and ladies of the night intermixed. Likewise, crime also was readily apparent.

Among the characters still locally touted today, partly because of his interesting demise, is James Butler Hickok, more popularly known as "Wild Bill" Hickok. An Illinois native, born in 1837, he came to notoriety, in part, by the many fables he created about himself. It is said that he played many roles during his lifetime—from actor and gambler to soldier and lawman—and, not surprisingly, he was involved in a number of gunfights. His death, however, did not come from a draw but from a cowardly shot in the back while playing cards on August 2, 1876, at a local saloon. His executioner, Jack McCall, also known as "Crooked Nose" or "Broken Nose Jack," was executed for the murder the following March. (See the story about Saloon No. 10 and a reenactment of Wild Bill's untimely death in the story preceding this one.)

Hickok's body was interred at Deadwood Cemetery, but his remains were later moved to Mount Moriah. It has been said that in a humorous twist of fate his body was placed next to Calamity Jane's, a rough-hewed female, born Martha Jane Canary, known for wearing bloomers, who supposedly had a crush on Hickok. She died due to inflammation of the bowels and pneumonia at the age of fifty-one on August 1, 1903, at the Calloway Hotel. "Wild Bill" never took an interest in Jane, it is said, but they nonetheless lie side by side in death.

As for the cards Hickok was holding when he died, they included a pair of black aces and eights—otherwise now known as the "dead man's hand." Kuchenbecker said Wild Bill's grave marker is one of his favorites—but noted there are many more interesting markers to observe and learn about at Mount Moriah. "Obviously, if you're an Old West enthusiast, seeing the grave of Wild Bill Hickok and Calamity Jane are pretty amazing—both legends in their own times," he said. "I personally like those. I've been to Buffalo Bill Cody's grave. I've been to Billy the Kid's grave. I've been to Doc Holliday's grave. Having Wild Bill at Mount Moriah right here in our own community is amazing and, for me personally, just being in charge of that cemetery is an honor."

He also explained: "We were involved with the reconstruction of a Chinese burner where early Chinese residents sent their fallen, their loved ones, into the afterlife through a ceremony, and all we had left was archaeological remains and photographs. We've done a complete reconstruction of that. Mount Moriah has an overlook of Deadwood and that's a beautiful place. But all in all, it's just tranquil; it's obviously sacred ground and means a lot to individuals who come here and obviously that's backed up with the number of visitors we get on an annual basis."

Most of the people who come to Mount Moriah today are interested in seeing where the famous and infamous are interred, these celebrities from the Old West; but sometimes people come here in the hopes of experiencing something from beyond the grave markers—to hear a voice, to feel a touch, to see a spirit.

Sometimes visitors are lucky—if that's what you want to call it—to actually experience what they came here in hopes of finding: the paranormal. For instance, it has been said that disembodied voices have been heard at the cemetery as have the sounds of children laughing. No children are visibly present when the laughter is heard, of course, leaving the door to mystery open. There is, however, a section where children are buried that could explain these phantom sounds—or at least adds to the mystery of the tale. There is also an area of mass graves.

Some believe Seth Bullock, founder of the namesake hotel in Deadwood, has returned from the grave to make sudden appearances from time to time. (It is rumored he also has been seen at his hotel.)

It is not uncommon to feel unnerved at a cemetery, especially an old one, and some people who have been to Mount Moriah claim to have felt as if they were being watched by unseen eyes. Whether it is their imagination from being in a graveyard or something more real, it is tough to tell unless one has experienced it for oneself.

Kuchenbecker said he has never experienced anything paranormal at the cemetery, but he has heard the stories, whether alleged or proven. One thing is for sure, a lot of living people visit Mount Moriah Cemetery every year. It is, in fact, one of Deadwood's most popular tourist attractions. The preservation office also hosts bus tours during the warm months, but the cemetery is open to visitors all year round. If you come here in winter, you'll definitely get chilled—but then you might at other times of the year as well, only in a different way, depending on your sensitivity to the spirit world.

When you plan a visit, the preservation office says it is best to allow a minimum of thirty minutes to view the celebrity graves. The site's visitor center also has a fifteen-minute interpretive video and other information about topics such as native and introduced plant species, cemetery symbolism, and death statistics within Deadwood from 1875 to 1900.

There's an old joke about cemeteries being popular places because "people are dying to get inside." But that's not the case at Mount Moriah. The newly deceased are no longer buried here—no bodies are interred here today—but all it costs for the living to pay a visit is $2 for a day pass.

As the preservation office reminds visitors, "Mount Moriah Cemetery is sacred place and should be treated with respect. Please take only photographs and leave nothing but memories."

THE PHANTOMS OF THE OPERA HOUSE

THE HOMESTAKE OPERA HOUSE, LEAD

An apparition appears on stage. Disembodied voices are heard in the hallways. Witnesses are many, the stories numerous. By these accounts, the Homestake Opera House in Lead, South Dakota, has been deemed one of the state's most haunted places.

Thomas Golden, executive director of the facility, said in a phone interview on April 15, 2022, that even though he has not personally witnessed anything supernatural at the early 1900s building, he nonetheless believes the stories—some which come from paranormal investigators who claim to have captured evidence of ghostly activity at the site. The most recent was from an investigation conducted in early 2022.

Built more than a century ago, in 1914, the Homestake Opera House is a venue for a number of performances throughout the year, from concerts, including classical and modern music, to hosting comedians and magic shows. "We try to bring in a nice, diverse set of performers, cross-cultural, bringing in things that people may not otherwise see," Golden said. "We try to give a good variety so people can see a lot here." The opera house was closed for a period of time beginning in 1984, seventy years after it initially opened, when a devastating fire destroyed much of the building. There it sat like a wounded beast, charred and lonely, until its reopening in 1998 when the city of Lead purchased the property and started renovations.

The ghosts came later.

Golden said of the mission of the opera house today: "We've got kind of a two-fold mission. We are a performing arts venue; we're trying to bring performing arts to the Black Hills community, emphasizing it as well, giving access to people who otherwise could not afford a night at the theater, or have access to the arts, through subsidized tickets." Through its educational programs it also offers scholarships "so people can be given access to the arts at every age, regardless of socioeconomic status. And then, because we have this wonderful historic building that is still unfinished in its restoration, we are committed to completing that restoration and bringing it back to its original glory of 1914."

The opera house opened that year, 1914, as a gift from Homestake Mine to the community of Lead, Golden said. Visitors would pay for a ticket, which admitted them to the show, but anything else in the building was free. That meant access to a billiards hall, bowling alley, library, and swimming pool. "It was just a major community center as well as being a state-of-the-art theater," he said. "We continue to be a central piece in the community in that way."

Money for the restoration, as with most any project, is always the big issue. He said he and his team are always trying to find new ways to fundraise for the restoration, noting it is an ongoing project that has experienced a lot of "starts and stops" along the way, but they hope to see major progress and near completion sometime over the next five years. "There's a lot of work that's been done and there is a lot of work left to do," he said. "I don't know that we have a real end in sight currently."

According to those in the know, paranormal activity often begins or ticks up during renovation projects. While there is no definitive reasoning for this, some believe it is because it disturbs the spirits' familiarity of their surroundings. Spirits often haunt a location because it meant something to them in real life and any adjustments to such places sometimes irritate the unseen entities, causing them to make their presences and displeasure known. Could that be why the paranormal activity happens at the Homestake Opera House?

It is a possibility.

Black Hills Paranormal Investigation, the group Golden said investigated the building, got back to him several months after their investigation of the facility, reviewing with him what they had found. I tried several times to contact the group, but to no avail. Golden said what was revealed during the investigation was that they had captured a number of electronic voice phenomena (EVPs).

During another investigation of the site some years earlier, in 2013, the group captured another batch of EVPs, according to a report written by Jaci Conrad Pearson in the October 31, 2013, *Black Hills Pioneer*. The spirits at that time also manifested themselves by some physical means—and not in a very nice way. For instance, team members were investigating near the facility's swimming pool, now capped over but still accessible, when they heard what sounded like rocks being thrown at them, even though no visible person was seen chucking the stones. "The first time they heard the sound of a rock hitting something, they questioned the validity of what had just happened," wrote Pearson. "Soon, a cry from one of the investigators validated their theory." One of the investigators had been hit by a rock, apparently thrown by a phantom.

"We've had some anecdotal tales of that as well outside of their group," Golden told me. "And they heard some voices up on the stage." He said the ghost stories are interesting—and though he believes people's stories about the ghosts that may roam his facility, he doesn't personally seek experiences with the unseen entities. He leaves that to the investigators and is content to only hear the stories. "I've worked all hours, late at night, and have never been the guy who sees or hears anything," Golden said. "That seems to just be my place. But we've had a performer who was in here rehearsing for a piano concert who said that she could hear someone, as if they were marching along with the music, and then when she stopped playing, the phantom footsteps stopped. A performer heading up from the dressing rooms heard someone say hi to him, but he was the only person there. We've had a few of those reports come through."

He said the tales, most which predate his arrival in 2021, attract the attention of others, some who visit in the hopes of sensing or seeing something unexplained. In that way, the ghost stories serve as a good marketing tool. "We do get people who come into the opera house who say, 'I'm specifically here because of the ghosts,'" Golden commented. "Sometimes they have information that even the staff has never heard about, different stories and different tales, and we're always interested because of the power that has to draw people in. We've talked a lot about it. . . . You don't want to make up stories out of nothing. You want to have something you can kind of grab onto, and those stories really do stir people's imaginations."

He said the ghost stories, as creepy as some of the experiences people have had here, help market the facility because many people come here in the hopes of experiencing a phantom at the opera house. "When people come here, they don't necessarily want to see a ghost, they just want to have the risk that they might, and that is powerful marketing. You really almost can't beat it," he said. "People are going to come to see a show, but there's kind of a swath of tourism that is, you know, I heard there's a ghost here. What can you tell me? . . . It's quiet marketing, because once in a while you'll have a paranormal investigation and there'll be a newspaper article about it and people will renew some interest. But those things, eventually they taper off a little and then it's just sort of quiet publicity; people may still be talking about it, but it's not at the forefront. It's not your major marketing push, but it's still very powerful."

UNSETTLING EXPERIENCES AT A PRIVATE RESIDENCE

STURGIS

Andrea Steele, a homeowner who has had a number of frightening experiences at her place of residence since moving there in late 2018, says she has dealt with the paranormal most of her life, including one incident she remembers vividly from when she was four years old. Over the past few years, she has had many experiences to add to her library of life. The chapters, however, have not been pleasant additions.

Steele shares a house with her partner, Dave, and children in Sturgis, South Dakota.

Within a year of moving into the mid-twentieth-century house, the family started experiencing strange, unnerving occurrences that, over time, escalated to physical attacks, in some instances. "The first year was pretty quiet," she said. But things started changing, as they did for the rest of the world with a global pandemic, in 2020. It started with little things, but then activity escalated, "and this past year it started getting really bad, people getting slapped and those kinds of things," she said during an interview in early 2022.

The modest home sits in a quiet neighborhood in a city of roughly seven thousand people. Steele is a nurse by profession and, ironically, the house used to belong to a patient she once took care of at the local hospital. Though she doesn't know for sure, she believes her patient and the woman's husband may be the ones haunting the abode. It is the husband's spirit she is frightened by.

The disturbances started with simple things, such as a door opening on its own. She'd go to close the door, only to return a few minutes later to find it open when she was the only one in the house. She'd also hear voices. Sometimes they sounded like children laughing, and she'd shrug it off as kids playing outdoors; other times she'd distinctly hear an adult's voice mumbling short phrases or incoherent words.

In sharing her stories, Steele explained that paranormal activity has been experienced through all parts of the house, including the basement, where she experienced one of her most frightening moments. She was restless one night and decided to go downstairs to sleep so she wouldn't disturb her partner and family upstairs. While on the sofa, she was startled from her slumber by a hard slap across the face. She arose from the couch, turned on the lights, and didn't see a living being anywhere in the room. "I have never been more afraid in my life," she said.

Another frightening experience happened in October 2021, while Steele was convalescing from COVID-19. She said she was terribly ill and was in bed for about twelve days. She would go through bouts of being hot, then chilled, and then hot again. She would put socks on her feet to keep them warm, but would intermittently pull them off. One time, she wore a pair of long socks to bed to keep her feet and legs warm. When she started to heat up, she went to remove the stockings and heard a loud, shattering explosion from the adjacent bathroom. Startled, she groggily dragged herself from bed to see what had happened.

All of the bathroom's light bulbs had exploded.

There was glass all over the place, she relayed, but at the time she was too weak to clean up the mess. It had to wait.

While these two experiences—being slapped in the face and the bulb explosion—were her most frightening experiences to date, there have been plenty of other disturbances that have unnerved Steele and her family. She said she has felt assaulted by unseen hands that have touched various parts of her body, sometimes in inappropriate places. She has felt pressure on her bed, as if someone were sitting down alongside her, and she has felt touching sensations on her head while showering.

Her partner and her children have also experienced paranormal activity at the home. Her daughter, for instance, claims to have experienced the heavy-handed slap of an unseen entity, and has woken during the wee hours of the night on several occasions to find a dark shadow figure standing by her bed. Dave had a toy thrown at him by unseen hands.

The big question Steele asks is, why are these things happening? She'd also like to know for sure who or what is making them happen. Steele said she has had various paranormal investigators, including Peggy Peters, founder of South Dakota Paranormal Investigations, visit her house to help find answers.

Before Peters visited the house, she asked that cameras be set up in parts of the home to record the alleged activity. One camera was set up in the master bedroom, and one night, as Steele and her partner slept, all seemed quiet and normal until she turned over in her bed. In her movement, she flipped the covers off of her and from beneath the sheets flew an orb. "That's when we knew there was something going on at the house," Peters said.

Later, when Peters visited the home for an investigation, she came to this conclusion: "She definitely has a presence there," Peters told me during a follow-up interview on July 20, 2022. "It was pretty active that night we were there." By the time we talked she and her team hadn't yet gone through all of their findings to come to a conclusion what might be haunting the abode. She did say, however, that they picked up at least three EVPs, one with a child crying and another that very clearly said "Get out!" Also, at one point during the investigation, lights in the kitchen started to flicker and flash, and large sliding doors shook on their sliders.

"There is something pretty strong in there," Peters said, though noting her team never did make direct contact with anything. Steele "believes it is a demon, but we're not sure because we didn't see anything that would indicate a malevolent presence," Peters continued. "But obviously her little girl is very scared."

Steele said she has witnessed with her natural eyes light coming down the stairs, and orbs have been captured in recordings from different parts of the house.

The investigations by paranormal groups, as well as Steele's own research and conversations with neighbors, have led her to believe that the home's former occupants may be the ones doing the haunting. She also said she was told by one group that, besides the adult presences in the house, there also are the spirits of several children in the residence who look upon her as a mother figure, a protector, and follow her around the home. This might explain why Peters caught the EVP of a child's crying spirit.

But does that mean something was done to the children in life for which they were afraid or hurt? The children's presences are not the frightening entities, Steele said; they are not the ones who slapped her. That attack came from an adult, likely a male figure, who Steele said likely had a sketchy past.

On the afternoon of April 22, 2022, when Steele related these experiences, she said that despite the disturbances, she likes her old house and doesn't have any plans of leaving anytime soon, partly because the price of property is so expensive. She has felt threatened by the slap and the exploding light bulbs, but she has become accustomed to most of the other activity.

Steele expects she'll always be haunted, just as she always has been since she was a little girl growing up in Williston, North Dakota. She was raised as a God-fearing Christian and never understood why she has been haunted, but she has accepted the fact that spirits seem to always be near. She doesn't mind the spirit children staying close to her, following her around the home, but Steele would like closure on the more unnerving aspects of the activity. "I do pray," she said. "But things keep happening. I think I'm just someone who is more open to it than other people."

WAILING SPIRITS

SOUTH UNIT OF THE BADLANDS NATIONAL PARK, INTERIOR

It is said that if you wander South Dakota's Badlands, there is a chance you might hear the wailing cries of Native Americans who lived here long ago. Those lingering spirits in the wild are not the prime attractions of this natural wonder, but if you do hear these restless spirits, it is definitely a bonus.

Both the Dakotas have their Badlands, but each have their own unique qualities and traits. The Badlands in the northern state are more mesa-looking, while South Dakota's Badlands are more conical, striped by light and dark hues of rust, orange, and pink. Both look primeval, as if dinosaurs still walk the terrain today. Look long enough and you might imagine a velociraptor scurrying around a bend. These are magnificent hills, prime for exploring by foot or mountain bike. Along your route, there's a chance you will encounter wildlife, for the expansive park system is home to many varieties of animals. In this unit, black-footed ferrets, bighorn sheep, bison, prairie dogs, pronghorn, and birds of prey make their home, as do a variety of other birds, amphibians, reptiles—including rattlesnakes and turtles—and a variety of butterflies.

They don't know this place as bad lands—for them it has always been good.

The name Badlands, according to information from the National Park Service, came from the Lakota tribe who called this wild and unruly place "mako sica," which translates to "bad lands." Likewise, when French fur trappers passed through the area in the 1800s, they called it "les mauvaises terres a traveser," meaning "bad lands to travel across."

But what made the area "bad"?

"The Badlands presents many challenges to easy travel. When it rains in the Badlands, the wet clay becomes slick and sticky, making it very difficult to cross," reads information from the Park Service. "The jagged canyons and buttes that cover the landscape also make it hard to navigate. The winters are cold and windy, the summers are hot and dry, and the few water sources that exist are normally muddy and unsafe to drink."

Challenges of living here aside, it is a great place to visit, something the tribes knew early on when they hunted these grounds.

The South Dakota Department of Tourism suggests parking at the White River Visitor Center at the southeast corner of the park and hiking west to Coffin Butte, a place within the unit with its own interesting name, believed to be named for its shape. "If so," the department says, "the title became a prophetic one after a skeleton was discovered in 1936 by a pastor and an intrepid group of Boy Scouts. The story behind the skeleton isn't clear—some think it's Ezra Kind, the last surviving member of a gold expedition, and others believe it was a Native American who ascended the butte to escape a pursuing posse—but questions like this only inspire fascination among intrepid explorers."

Does the ghost of this person appear as an apparition? It is a fun possibility to consider, but there is also the tale of the wailing spirits who are most often heard at night. It is also rumored that on occasion the spirits might manifest themselves by more than only sound. Legend says that Native warriors have been known to appear, riding their horses, whooping into the night air before vanishing into the netherworld from whence they came.

The South Unit of the Badlands, the department of tourism says, is an often-overlooked unit of the park system but one where mysteries and intrigue abound. It has lots of nature and fun things to explore. Add it to your travel list, but do be careful when exploring the park, whether in daylight or after the sky turns dark. Don't turn into a ghost yourself, and make safety your first priority.

There is camping here, too. Check with the park for current pricing information, for day passes, camping, and motorized vehicle fees. To get to the unit, take Exit 191 on Interstate 90 for the northeast entrance; the Pinnacles entrance is accessed at Exit 110 from Interstate 90. From Interior, take Highway 44 to Highway 377.

Welcome to the Badlands!

THE SOUL GATHERER: A TALE OF WALKING SAM

PINE RIDGE INDIAN RESERVATION, MANDERSON-WHITE HORSE CREEK

Among the many ghost stories of the Dakotas—those who go on record to share their experiences with the paranormal—there are also a number of folktales and urban legends. This book, while relying heavily on input from real people, also shares some of those tales passed around in paranormal circles. One of them is about a frightening figure that stalks weary victims in the Pine Ridge Indian Reservation in the southwest region of South Dakota.

The figure, described as appearing much like the notorious Slenderman of social media and film fame, haunts his weary victims—those who are downtrodden and depressed—by messing with their minds. He whispers to them in subtle ways, telling them that they have used up their lives and they no longer have any purpose. Why not end it? he urges, prompting them to end their pain once and for all by completing suicide. He then gathers these souls unto himself, like medals won from battle, becoming stronger by his victims' loss of life. In this way he also is much like a vampire, who finds strength from its victims' blood.

The name of the deplorable entity is "Walking Sam," because he wanders the Indian reservation of the Oglala Lakota, searching for his next victim. He walks and walks, never tiring in his search for new victims. Sadly, many have listened to his nonsensical temptations. His success can be tracked by the number of people who have attempted self-harm or died by suicide on the reservation over the years.

Walking Sam, described as being some seven feet tall, with long limbs and no mouth, is most frightening when he stretches out his arms, elongating them to their full capacity. It is then, with his outstretched limbs as if reaching for the netherworld from which he came, that one can see the souls of his victims hanging from his arms like trophies. The haunting scene does not in any way replicate a mother hen who has gathered her chicks under her wings to provide shelter and warmth; no, this is an evil monstrosity from the darkest side of existence who is showcasing his nefarious work.

The Walking Sam story has been around for a number of years, but it is unknown how the tale came to be.

EASTERN AND
CENTRAL
SOUTH DAKOTA

A DAY AT THE MUSEUM

THE PETTIGREW HOME & MUSEUM, SIOUX FALLS

It is rumored that at least one ghost—but maybe several—haunt the Pettigrew Home & Museum, located at 131 North Duluth Avenue in Sioux Falls. The two-story building—which also has an attic and basement not open to the public—was built by Thomas and Jenny McMartin in 1889, but is named after Richard Franklin Pettigrew, who purchased the property in the early 1900s and set it upon the path to its present life as a museum.

Pettigrew, born July 23, 1848, in Ludlow, Vermont, came to the Dakota Territory in 1869. A lawyer and land surveyor by trade, Pettigrew was best known for his congressional work, first representing the territory and then in the Senate after South Dakota was admitted to the Union in 1889, the very year that the McMartins built their home. He was the first senator to represent South Dakota, and by all accounts Pettigrew was passionate about Sioux Falls and his adopted state. "He was responsible for bringing in all five early railroads, developing many businesses for the community," reads an entry on the museum's webpage. He served two terms as the state's senator and championed "the rights of women, farmers, and the common working man."

He was also a world traveler and avid collector, a trait that seems to have served him well when he decided to open a museum. When the McMartin house caught his attention in 1911, the encounter set in motion what one day would become a historic site. He purchased the property, lived in the house for a number of years, and added on to it in 1923, creating a two-story museum. Two years later, in 1925, he incorporated a museum of natural history on the property.

Sadly, Pettigrew died only a year after the museum opened, but before his passing, he willed the property and his collections to the city of Sioux Falls—with one request: "He asked the city to continue operating the museum," said Carolyn Johnson, museum interpreter at the Siouxland Heritage Museums, which manages the property. "From there, there was some legalese to sort out. Some people said the city should not accept this gift, that there's no legal basis for it. But ultimately, on January 1, 1930, the city officially accepted that building and the property there. We've been a city museum ever since."

In about 1933 or 1934, Johnson explained, the city added another addition to the museum on the side of the house to have more space, not only for Pettigrew's artifacts but also for those items that people had donated over the years. At one time, from 1930 to about 1973, the museum's curators lived in an adjacent section of the house. "They were living in the house, running the museum in the back of the house, and it was in the 1980s that the house went through a big restoration project," she said. "And so now we operate the historic house that people see on the tour, and there's the museum gallery as well."

Who knows if any of the curators over the years experienced disturbances at the property? But Johnson, who had been in her post for eight years by the time we talked on June 1, 2022, said she had not experienced anything that she would classify as paranormal. She has heard the stories, however, some of which she said have been passed down for years. Those stories include the phantom odor of women's perfume—which seems to all of a sudden permeate areas of the residence without warning, and then dissipating just as abruptly—and the visage of a young child reportedly seen without its mortal cloak.

"I admit I'm a little bit of a skeptic, but the house does creak and groan," she told me, noting sometimes a door once closed might be found ajar when no one else had entered the room. "But I tend to chalk that up to being forgetful—and it's an old house."

Another strange happening she has heard about is lights that turn on by themselves with no apparent explanation as to why. "There are some stories out there about somebody closing everything down and locking the house, turning all the lights off and leaving, and then driving by hours later and seeing a light on in the attic," she said. "The person goes back to turn off the lights, drives away, and comes back later to find the light back on." The origin of the stories and to whom the prankster spirits might belong are unknown, Johnson said, but if there are unseen entities visiting the site, it has been rumored that the perfumed spirit may be that of Jenny McMartin, the first lady of the home.

The Pettigrew Home and Museum is open all year and free to the public, but its hours change depending on the season. Visitors may take self-guided tours through the museum, where they will see Pettigrew's many collections as well as items that other people have donated through the years. There is also a twenty-minute guided tour of the house, which is decorated with period furnishings thanks to the 1980s restoration project. The effort was to make the site resemble what it may have looked like during Pettigrew's tenure in the home.

The mystery of the alleged spirits remains, but thankfully so does the tangible history of the house. The Pettigrew Home and Museum is a pleasant place to visit where one can learn a little about the property's past, including tidbits about Sioux Falls history, and see what it was like for one of the state's earliest legislators to live and function amid 1900s splendor.

"I think the best thing really is touring the house and for people to actually see what it was like for a wealthy person living in Sioux Falls 100 years ago," Johnson said. "Everybody takes different things away from that. Whether it's them saying, 'Oh, wow, look at the stained-glass windows!' or learning about the maids, it's really just seeing what life was like for people in the house."

A STATELY, POSSIBLY HAUNTED BUILDING

THE OLD COURTHOUSE MUSEUM, SIOUX FALLS

Not far from the Pettigrew Home and Museum is the Old Courthouse Museum, located at 200 West 6th Street in Sioux Falls. It is a magnificent building known for its architecture—a testament to its time and place in history.

There may be some spirits that linger here, too.

The year 1889 seems to be a popular date in South Dakota history. It was then that statehood was achieved and significant events occurred and buildings were developed—such as, in this case, the original Minnehaha County Courthouse. It was completed in 1893 and housed all of the elements of county government for nearly seventy years, until 1962, when a new and larger courthouse was built. "By that point, they had run out of space in the courthouse," said Carolyn Johnson, museum interpreter. At the time of its construction, however, Wallace L. Dow, the architect of the building, claimed it would be the "largest courthouse between Chicago and Denver."

Once the new courthouse opened, Dow's building sat vacant for about ten years before it started to take on a new life in more modern times. Despite the modernity all around it, the facility would beckon to the past as a museum. "The county wasn't sure what to do with it. They were strongly considering tearing the building down to put a parking lot here," Johnson said. "But ultimately, they came together with this idea of making the courthouse another museum for the area—again, kind of focused on local and regional history."

Local residents who saw the value of keeping the old building worked to save it from demolition, and in 1974, it was converted into a museum, the second in a trio of properties as part of the Siouxland Heritage Museums, an umbrella organization that was formed in 1974. The other historic site is the Pettigrew Home and Museum, which Wallace also designed (as well as the South Dakota State Penitentiary and All Saints School), and the Irene Hall Museum Resource Center houses artifacts not on exhibit at the two museums.

"I spend about half my time at both of those buildings," Johnson said of the Pettigrew Home and Museum and the Old Courthouse Museum. "The two buildings are about five blocks apart, so they're kind of independent when you're visiting them, but we operate jointly in conjunction with one another." She said an ongoing restoration project over the years has been done to make the latter building look like the original courthouse.

Both the facade and interior of the old courthouse still fascinates with its construction of Sioux Quartzite stone, while inside are granite pillars, stained-glass windows, and tiled fireplaces. "Perhaps one of the most striking features of the building is the 16 large murals on the walls of the hallways painted between 1915 and 1917," according to information from the Heritage Museums. "Painted by Norwegian immigrant Ole Running, the murals detail early life in Dakota, natural features, and images of his home in Norway. Running was paid $500 for his work on the walls of the building."

Johnson said there are not as many ghost tales associated with the courthouse as there are with the Pettigrew sites. But there are a few, including those about noises that sound as if the elevator is moving up and down when no one else is in the building.

While here, look upward—to the clock tower. What do you see?

"There's people who say they've seen a person up on top of the clock tower," Johnson said, noting there is also a story about a spectral janitor, broom in hand, who continues his work "sweeping throughout the building."

Johnson said all of the tales she's heard about the building have been passed down, nothing personal that really substantiates the claims of ghosts. "I don't know a single person who has said they have seen or felt anything in the courthouse," she said, but noted the stories are interesting.

Johnson did, however, say this about the building: "I think the building is very beautiful outside and inside. That surprises a lot of people; our modern-day courthouses are pretty utilitarian. But this one has murals on the walls through-out the first and second floors. The offices have decorative friezes and the ceilings are painted and adorned. There's woodwork and wrought iron railings on the staircases; and the outside has a big clock tower that's just kind of a showpiece."

SNEAKY LITTLE DEVILS

SPIRIT MOUND, VERMILLION

Located not quite seven miles north of Vermillion, in Clay County, is a prominent hill that in the 1800s was feared by members of the First Nation tribe.

Why they feared such a pleasant hill seems odd today, but according to the stories they had good reason to be suspicious, even fearful, of the mound. For unknown reasons, the tribe had for a long time believed that the hill had inhabitants with special powers. In an attempt to remove them from the vicinity, a band of warriors went up against them one day but found no success in their efforts. Instead, they found death.

The warriors were driven out and killed by the mound's inhabitants, cunning little people whom the First Nation peoples believe wielded crafty, magical weapons. The massacre cemented the belief of the tribe that the mound was indeed a place they shouldn't venture to for fear of the menacing spirits, or little devils, whom they believed occupied it—they and their craft.

In some stories the devils were little indeed, being only some eighteen inches tall.

In other stories, explorer Pierre La Vérendrye, who traveled through the area in the mid-1700s, called the mound the "Dwelling of the Spirits" and reported seeing sparkling stones and gold-colored sand on the hill.

Today, Spirit Mound Historic Prairie, managed by the South Dakota Department of Game, Fish, and Parks, is a nice, though perhaps dull, place to visit. There's not much to see here—except a view of the pleasant valley beyond the green prairie grass. There is a trail, about a half-mile long, to hike and opportunities for picnicking and birdwatching. The Vermillion River passes through the area as well. After visiting, standing atop this mound in prairieland, one can say she or he has stood in the very spot where Meriwether Lewis and William Clark stood more than a century ago during their now-famous Corps of Discovery Expedition.

When Lewis and Clark came to Dakota Territory, they met with Native tribes along their route, and learned from the locals of the belief that little devils inhabited the hill. Their curiosity piqued, Lewis and Cark set off for the mound on August 25, 1804, finding not any little people or devils but a herd of grazing buffalo. According to information from the South Dakota Game, Fish, and Parks Department, "In order to provide Spirit Mound visitors with an opportunity similar to what Lewis and Clark experienced, the site is being restored." The restoration started in 2021 and "prairie grasses and other native plants are being reestablished." It's not an overnight task, though, and one that will take decades of growth to restore it to its rightful splendor: "Spirit Mound has a rich variety of prairie wildflowers and grasses and is home to Fritillary butterflies, birds and many other prairie animals."

The coy and cunning little devils can keep their magical arrows to themselves, thank you very much. Instead, go here to have encounters with nature.

JESSE JAMES, A NATIVE AMERICAN LEGEND, AND PHANTOM SCREAMS

DEVIL'S GULCH, GARRETSON

The name Jesse James, one of America's most infamous outlaws of the 1800s, is well known in Wild West history and lore. But James wasn't confined to the West only. His wanderings took him across the country, including through parts of Dakota Territory to the red quartzite canyons and the eighteen-foot gorge of Devil's Gulch in present-day Garretson, South Dakota, where he allegedly jumped a footbridge in an attempt to flee from lawmen. Other stories of the Gulch are more ghostly and speak of phantom screams and dark shadows.

Located near the Minnesota border, Garretson is a small town, not quite 1,500 people by 2020 estimates, in Minnehaha County. Devil's Gulch, also known as Spirit Canyon, is one of the things that has put it on the map, at least for those with an interest in the outdoors and paranormal. It is a beautiful place to visit, with nearby Spirit Creek that flows some fifty-five miles among the natural rustic beauty of the area. Here, "cedar trees and bushes cling to the quartzite walls for life," Jeanne Richardson wrote in *South Dakota Magazine*. "Even to the unimaginative, Devil's Gulch is a vaguely ominous place; its name derives from the eerie noises that come from its bowels as the winds blow through. Within the gulch the water lies oily and motionless, except for an occasional gurgle of life, but it is said that powerful currents rage below the surface. Some areas are reported to be bottomless."

From time to time in my research, I have run across stories that tell of certain bodies of water, deep lakes and crevices in which no bottom has been detected. Often these stories are not scientifically based but presumed because of legends surrounding the site. In the case of Devil's Gulch, it is said that a group of local residents once dropped a six-hundred-foot line into the water below and didn't detect a bottom.

A Native American legend might give the story even more folklore merit. According to the story, a warrior named Ha-Shootch-Ga challenged Iktomi to a tomahawk duel. When one is challenged to duel, one cannot back out without being branded a coward. Iktomi accepted the challenge and the combatants met in the vicinity of the present-day Gulch. When it was Iktomi's turn, he lifted his tomahawk, sending it heavenward. When it eventually fell back to Earth, its impact created what they later termed "Spirit Canyon." As for Ha-Shootch-Ga, he apparently fled from Ikotomi's power and was never seen again.

Today, there's a wooden sign in the shape of South Dakota that welcomes visitors to the site. With its hand-painted scrawl, it reads: "DEVILS GULCH, HOME OF BEAUTY MYSTERY & LEGEND." A fitting description of the site, because each quality it lists—its beauty, mystery, and legends—seems to have intrigued people for a long time and continue to do so today. The Gulch is accessed off Main Street and 5th Street in Garretson.

As for the ghost stories of the site, one is about young lovers who died at the Gulch but whose spirits have never left. The alleged spirits date back to the 1800s, when a young woman was kidnapped by a band of outlaws who took her to the Gulch. Her fiancé learned of her abduction and went in haste to rescue her, but not before battling with the kidnappers and himself sustaining mortal wounds. Legend has it that he killed the kidnappers, but the feat cost him his life. The young woman whom he was to marry also died in the attack.

It is said that even today, moaning and deathly screams can be heard echoing across time and through the Gulch, repeating the haunting activity that took place here more than a century ago.

A PARANORMAL HISTORY

BERTON MORAN OF LOCAL LEGENDS, MITCHELL

An old woman walks from one upstairs room to another, startling the home's occupants. Over time the homeowners become accustomed to the woman's unexpected appearance, for it happens almost every day; but for family friends who visit the house, it is always a shock to encounter her ghost.

"Who is that?" one house guest asks the homeowner after seeing a woman complete her daily routine. "I didn't know you had your mother-in-law staying with you."

"Oh, that's not my mother-in-law," says the homeowner. "That's our resident ghost."

The friend chuckles, waiting for the punchline of the joke. But this is no joke.

"You don't believe me?" the homeowner asks. When the answer is apparent, he says: "Go take a look for yourself."

The visitor trundles up the stairs, going into the room he saw the woman enter. It is empty, and there is no exit except for the single door that the visitor just used, the same door he saw the woman walk through.

Realizing this is the punchline—that there really is a resident ghost at the old house—the visitor stumbles back down the stairs, goose pimples likely still running up the back, and tells the homeowner it is time to leave. The visitor doesn't want to remain in a haunted house.

The paranormal that Berton Moran has experienced throughout his life started with the spirit of an old woman haunting his childhood home—and the experiences haven't stopped yet. Moran, based in Mitchell, says he is not sure why the paranormal has followed him the way it has, but it is something he has gotten accustomed to—as much as a person can get used to being tagged by ghosts and shadow figures.

His experience with the paranormal began when he was a child, living with his siblings and parents in their home in White River, South Dakota, part of the Rosebud-Sioux Indian Reservation in the southwestern portion of the state. His father owned a junkyard and their home sat on the same property. His parents would often entertain friends, welcoming them into their home for coffee and good conversation. Moran remembers that home well, for it was where the ghostly apparition of a woman appeared time and again on the second floor, walking with her phantom legs from the upstairs bathroom to a bedroom, and back again, before disappearing.

"All my life I've had to deal with spirits," Moran said in a phone conversation on June 25, 2022. "But yeah, in that one we had an elderly woman." His experiences with the paranormal may have started with the phantom old lady, but that was just the tip of the proverbial iceberg. His experiences continue to this day. Now a father, he says the paranormal has made itself known to his children.

Because he has had so many experiences with unseen presences—and some of them seen, like the old woman—he decided he should pay attention. When he became of age, he started to investigate and today produces a number of videos about the paranormal and other strange phenomena on his YouTube channel, *Local Legends*. It is a part-time gig, more of a hobby than anything else, that he runs out of his home office. Of course, before he puts videos together, he first gathers evidence at the many places he visits throughout the year.

Moran shared several experiences he's had with South Dakota's darker side, including the ghost of a playful little boy, and his most frightening experience with a dark and vengeful entity, possibly a demon.

LITTLE BOY GHOST, WHITE RIVER

"I remember I was doing my homework in the living room of the same house [where the phantom lady would appear] one afternoon," he said. "I looked down the hallway and see this little boy poking his head out, staring at me. . . . It wasn't uncommon for my parents to have a lot of guests over to drink coffee, and if they had little kids, it was usually my job to take them into the living room to watch cartoons and entertain them so the adults could talk. I figured, OK, I'll bring the kid back here with me.

"I go out to the kitchen, where my mom is doing dishes. I look around, but don't see the kid." He asked his mom who all is in the house. She replied that it was just the two of them at the moment; his dad had gone into town and his brother was at a friend's house.

Moran then asked who the kid was, but his mom didn't know what he was talking about. "What kid?" she replied.

"The kid that was just staring at me?"

"Yeah, there is no kid," she said.

A TERRIFYING EXPERIENCE, RAPID CITY

Moran said the most terrifying experience he's had happened while going to college in Rapid City. He was at his aunt and uncle's house at the time, and said the activity he witnessed there one day, even after everything else that he had experienced, threw him for a loop.

"My parents used to foster a lot of children," he said. "We had a group of kids staying with us—about the same age as I was—and there was a kid I grew up very attached to. . . . As he got older and had to go back to the state . . . I heard that he ended up committing suicide. . . . I was very close with him at the time, and it very much upset me. I was eighteen, had moved out of my parents' house, deciding to go to school up in Rapid City for a while. And my mother gave me a call and informed me of what happened, and it very much broke my heart, I was very upset."

He was at his aunt's house doing laundry in the basement when he received the disturbing phone call. He threw the laundry across the room and broke down in tears. He tried to compose himself before going back upstairs, where his aunt, cousin, and some friends were hanging out. When he finally made the trek upstairs, the group could see that something was visibly wrong. The cousin and friends went into the back room, and Moran stayed with his aunt, who asked what was wrong. Moran told her, and his aunt tried to comfort him. But Moran felt another presence in the room.

"I don't know if you've ever had that feeling of somebody staring at you across the room, like they want to kick your butt," he said. "But I got that feeling. I tell my aunt the story, and she looks very concerned about what I'm telling her."

Then Moran asked her: "'Do you ever get that feeling as if somebody is staring at you?'

"And her face of sadness turned to one of concern." She inquired where he felt that someone was staring at him. "I point to the kitchen, and as soon as I do that, she turns her head, looks into the kitchen—and the cupboard doors open and dishes started flying off the shelves. The doors are opening—basically all hell broke loose inside her kitchen."

Moran was frightened, but his aunt "very calmly stands up and walks over to a wooden box that she has on a bookshelf, pulls out some sage and burns it, and starts walking into the kitchen. Whatever it was, she ushers it down the stairs into the basement."

Then she asked Moran if the basement is where he got upset a few minutes before. "I said I did. Then she said, 'you got his attention.'" Moran didn't know what she meant, and so he asked. His aunt's response: "Whatever it is, it lives in the basement, and waits for people to get upset; it feeds off their emotions."

"I was like, what is this thing?" Moran explained. "And she said, all she could think of is that it was a demon.

"That was terrifying. I was like, 'Oh, I'm ready to get out of this house.' But as I got older and remembered the stories and all the things that have happened, I knew I needed to investigate [the paranormal] because stuff keeps happening. Ghost hunting is something I've always been interested in, ever since it came looking for me. Now, I'm looking for it."

THE ISLAND OF LOST SOULS

LA FRAMBOISE ISLAND NATURE PRESERVE, PIERRE

Yes, even the Great Plains are home to an island. Check out La Framboise Island in Pierre, South Dakota, for a jaunt through nature and history—including para-history. The island, which goes by a few different names, is apparently home to a few ghosts.

Meriwether Lewis and William Clark, during their Corps of Discovery Expedition in 1804, visited the island, with Clark giving it one of its nicknames: Bad Humor Island. While trying to meet with Native Americans here, showing them their boat, the Natives soon gave them some trouble, according to Clark's journal, after which they "proceeded on about 1 mile & anchored out off a Willow Island," he wrote (original spelling intact), noting further, "I call this Island bad humered Island as we were in a bad humer."

Another name for it is just the opposite of bad: Good Humor Island.

Berton Moran, of the *Local Legends* YouTube channel, commented on the twin names that seem to be at odds with each other: "There's quite a bit of history to it. . . . I've read it multiple ways online—they nicknamed it good humor island because when they first appeared they saw some wildlife and they thought, 'Oh, it's a beautiful place. Let's call it Good Humor Island.' But they also ran into some trouble with the Natives, and they wrote about it in the journal but didn't specify what kind of trouble they ran into. And from that experience, they also named it bad humor island."

Moran has visited the island several times and, at the time we spoke, wants to go back. It is a very active place, he said.

During his visits, Moran said he has heard phantom footsteps following him on a trail and heard voices in the woods. During one visit, as the sounds approached, Moran looked back to see who was following him and no one was there. This is in line with other reported accounts of people walking along the trail hearing what sounds like footsteps following them. Voices heard when no one else is in sight also is a common attribution to the site. Moran said, "Multiple people—a lot of people—have talked to me about what they've experienced. . . . They'd be out on these trails at night or early morning, and they'll hear whispering, right behind them. And of course, you're out on the island in the middle of nowhere. . . . A lot of people claim to have heard that."

During one visit that Moran filmed, featured in his video "Haunted Island (Pierre, SD)" (https://www.youtube.com/watch?v=3-vcRpKhucs), Moran said he had one of his most unexpected experiences: "I was walking back . . . and heard somebody rush up behind me like a full-on sprint, running directly behind me. I turned around so fast that I just about fell on myself, because I thought somebody was trying to run into me. I turn around and there's nothing there. It was very interesting, because, like I said, it sounded like somebody was running a dead sprint straight at me."

The hauntings at this island are not confined to noise only. Stories say the spirit of a little girl is reported to make an appearance from time to time, seeking help from the island's mortal visitors. It is not known to whom the spirit of the little girl belongs, but Moran said it could be from one who drowned at the site.

The island sits in the midst of the Missouri River. "It's kind of a sad situation out there," he said. "About every year somebody ends up drowning. A lot of the time the current will take them and the bodies can't be found for a few days, and then wash up on shore or farther into Pierre," Moran said, noting he's heard reports of people dying of heart attacks or other maladies while at the island. "Stuff like that happens all the time."

Whether the spirits of these individuals remain—or return—to haunt the place of their demise is obviously not known, but these firsthand experiences add to the para-history of the island.

A TALE OF MANY GHOSTS

FORT SISSETON HISTORIC STATE PARK, LAKE CITY

Ali Tonsfeldt has gotten used to the ghosts at Fort Sisseton Historic Park. During our conversation on July 15, 2022, she told me that there are many, and she has had encounters with several of them. She's not the only one.

Tonsfeldt, park manager, said when she first came on board, she was a bit of a skeptic. Ghost stories were interesting—and she'd heard about the spirits that supposedly haunted the historic park—but she didn't give the stories much credit as being true. And then she had her own experience with a spirit, changing her beliefs about the paranormal. "My gosh, we have so many ghost stories," she said. "We have ghost stories going back to the 1940s and 1950s."

Perhaps the most famous ghost at the park is that of the "Lady in White." Many places across the country, and around the globe, have stories of alleged women in white who haunt locales in dimly lit corridors, stairways, and grave-yards. But this park's Lady in White is all the rage for those who have seen her. The Lady in White, who has been reported at various locations of the property, has been seen for a number of years, but the site's restoration project in recent years increased the ghost activity, according to Tonsfeldt.

The Lady in White appears most often as a transparent figure wearing an old Victorian dress. Her favorite haunt seems to be the upstairs window of the Commander's House. Here, she is seen wearing the nightgown of a servant, a candle in her hands. It is believed the woman in this residual haunting is trying to burn bed bugs off the walls. Tonsfeldt explained to me that this was a nightly activity for a period of time in the 1870s. The fort was infested with bed bugs, and the women who worked in the commanding officer's house, every night, would take candles and burn the bedbugs off the room's walls before the commander retired to bed for the night.

A woman dressed in white, believed to be the same ghostly figure, has also been seen walking to the officers' quarters. And in a more public display, she has been known to appear on the boardwalk during festivals, seemingly oblivious that she is a main attraction, and where many may catch a fleeting glimpse of the apparition who lived and worked here long ago. Tonsfeldt said a man who had worked the festivals for about fifteen years encountered the apparition one day when he was on the boardwalk.

Tonsfeldt shared another experience from a staff member that happened in 2022. The member was painting in the Commander's House and felt what he thought was a cobweb on him. He swiped it away, but felt it again on his shoulder. He looked up and saw the Lady in White pass right in front of him. "She swept one side to the other in the stairwell that he was painting," she said, recounting his story. "It was kind of funny because we told him about our ghosts, but he never really believed. But now he does."

She said one time a little girl very badly wanted to stay to see if she could catch a glimpse of the Lady in White, who often is seen at around 3 in the morning. The park gave the girl and her dad permission to stay. As they waited outside the Commander's House, at about 3:35 a.m. the hoped-for phantom finally made her appearance. Her dad had dozed off, but the girl woke him with the exciting news, "She's here! She's here!" Tonsfeldt said it wasn't the park having someone play dress-up to serve the little's girl's wishes, it was the actual Lady in White, which she said most often appears transparent.

Tonsfeldt said other famous ghosts at the site are those of the Buffalo Soldiers, members of the Twenty-Fifth Infantry, who received that name because, when their hair was cut short, it resembled the fur of a buffalo. She said it was these soldiers who left the greatest mark on the guardhouse, where names of the builders are inscribed. She said an early experience she had with the paranormal at the site was when a Buffalo Soldier appeared to her.

"My first experience was only two weeks after I started working," she said. "My office desk faced the wall and so my back was to my door. I was working on some paperwork at about 10 o'clock at night. And you know when you get that feeling like somebody is behind you? I had that feeling and knew I wasn't the only person there. I turned around and there was a Buffalo Soldier standing right behind me at the door of my office, just staring at me." Tonsfeldt said the figure didn't stay long, but she took the experience as her cue to leave for the night.

She's had other experiences at the site as well, including one involving an old wind-up clock that hadn't worked for twenty years that, during renovation at the property, all of a sudden started ticking. She said it worked for seven hours. The next day when she asked the spirit to make its presence known by making the clock work again, the old timepiece again started counting the seconds.

Located in Lake City about thirty miles from Sisseton, Fort Sisseton came into existence in 1864 when a volunteer infantry from Wisconsin, led by General John Pope, established Fort Wadsworth in an effort to combat local Sioux with whom they contended. It was a contentious time, as one skirmish after another seemed to heat up the plains. A conflict between the whites and the Sioux in 1862, stretching across the Dakota Territory, prompted a number of forts to be built. Pope named the establishment Fort Wadsworth, but after learning there already was another fort by that name, it was changed to Fort Sisseton after the predominant Sioux tribe in the region.

Using local material, the fort was built with barracks and officers' quarters, a livery and powder house, and a house for the fort's commanding officer. It was an active and useful fort for the next two decades, providing shelter and work for both men and women, from soldier and blacksmith to laundress and maid. It was used as a military post and waystation for pioneers and others on their way to other points in the country; but eventually, as conflicts with the Sioux wound down, activity at the fort also died down. By 1889—the same year that South Dakota became a state—the army abandoned the fort, a scenario that played itself out, at one time or another, at the government's other forts.

Life and activity on the plains were changing.

The following year, the State of South Dakota obtained ownership of the fort, but little was done with it for nearly fifty years. It was used as a hunting lodge for a time before the Works Progress Administration stepped in to provide funding in 1937 to revitalize it. The fourteen surviving buildings began to regain their purpose—or, more accurately, they began to take on new purposes.

Fort Sisseton was designated a South Dakota Historic State Park in 1959 and was added to the National Register of Historic Places in 1973. Later, in the 1990s, it was used as a workplace for inmates. Tonsfeldt said that over all of the decades the fort has been in existence, it has never stopped playing an important part in the plains.

The fort, which sits on thirty-five acres, is open all year, but campers be forewarned that showers, flush toilets, and water systems may be closed from October through April.

In about the third weekend of May, people may get in free, thanks to South Dakota's offer of "free weekend" to its state park visitors. That's the beginning of the busy season, Tonsfeldt informed me.

In October, the site becomes even more ghostly as it celebrates the Halloween spirit with stories about the haunted fort. There also are some modern activities to enjoy, such as boating, walleye fishing, cabin camping, and outdoor trails to explore. There's also the popular Fort Sisseton Historical Festival, held every year during the first week of June since 1977—except for a period of time during the height of the coronavirus pandemic—that draws thousands of people every year. It is at this time when the Lady in White is often seen on the boardwalk, and if one didn't know any better, one might think she is part of the festival, dressed in her period clothing, as did the staff member who encountered her here during an event one year.

It also is believed that there is a little ghost boy who will sometimes escort visitors along the parade grounds late in the evening. He seems eager to associate and play with other children who come to the site but is saddened that he cannot. Tonsfeldt said the little boy ghost has been seen numerous times, sometimes catching people unaware and making believers out of them. The boy, who is dressed in 1900s clothing rather than 1800s, appeared once to an employee who heard the stories about the boy but didn't believe in spirtis. One night, he went to his car and, when he turned on the headlights, the apparition was right there, standing in front of his vehicle. "It's kind of funny," Tonsfeldt said, "because nobody believes in ghosts—and then they come to Fort Sisseton."

NATIVE AMERICANS AND THE SPIRIT WORLD

SISSETON AND ABERDEEN

The cry of a banshee.

That's one way to describe what Peggy Peters heard while visiting an abandoned schoolhouse near Aberdeen.

It wasn't her first encounter with the paranormal. Peters has had many, but notes she views such experiences differently than perhaps do more traditional spirit seekers. She thanks her Native heritage for that, which has given her a broad understanding of what the term "paranormal" might mean. Primarily, she focuses on the latter half of that word. It is "normal" to have spirits walk the earth among the living because they are, in essence, a part of this planet as much as any mortal. After all, they once were donned with flesh and blood, too.

It is tough to determine how many experiences with the unseen world Peters has had, but they are many and started long ago. Those experiences prompted her to start South Dakota Paranormal Investigations, and she and her team—which include members of her own family—investigate ghostly activity across the state.

They approach investigations differently than other traditional groups. As a Native American and member of the Sisseton tribe, she said her people do not believe in a heaven or a hell; they do not believe that spirits who make themselves manifest are trapped in this world and are trying to get out. Peters and her group do not try to help the spirits "go toward the light" or to move on to another existence, because they don't need to. They are a part of this world where they once lived as mortals. This earth is their eternal abode. "We believe human spirits can cross between the worlds of the living and the deceased," she said in a virtual interview on the evening of March 18, 2022. "They'll interact, they want to interact, and we don't go into [an investigation] with the mindset that we need to help these spirits get somewhere." "It's because we believe so strongly that the spirit world is always [here]," she said in a follow-up interview a few months later, on June 20, 2022. "It's their choice to go back and forth." Sometimes when a place is deemed haunted, she said, it may be the spirit of a family member who still remains in the home or has come back for a visit.

Like mortals, Peters said there are good spirits and bad spirits—which may account for the reasons a person might feel threatened by a paranormal entity. Some are just downright mean.

Peters has become more grounded in her beliefs of the paranormal since she started her investigations into the unseen world. She has seen what she calls "light spears"—streaks of light that she explained are the manifestation of a spirit entity. Light spears are most likely nonhuman spirits that manifest themselves in this way. They are quite common, she said, "but a lot of people miss them because they don't know about them. One of the reasons I believe that we [her team] get so much activity, that we have so many positive experiences, is that we come at it from a non-biblical train of thought or mindset." Meaning, at least in part, that they do not have an agenda when they investigate a residence, except to bring answers to the individuals and families whose homes are allegedly haunted.

Spirits and other "entities," as Peters calls them, may manifest themselves as orbs and make themselves known by appearing very real, even down to the apparent clothing with which they seem to be adorned. Of such spirits, she said: "They don't necessarily manifest as an aura or a shadow . . . they may look like an everyday person." Someone may notice such a visage and not realize that what they are seeing is a spirit. The unwary eyewitness may say, "Gee, that woman must really love vintage clothing. She's wearing these vintage clothes and they don't realize that it might actually be a spirit standing there.

"That's how we want to approach it," Peters explained. "That's how we do approach it."

As for that banshee cry, Peters said there are a number of ways spirits and other unseen entities communicate. Some ways are subtle, others more jarring. Of the latter, Peters remembers one experience quite well. She and her daughter once visited an abandoned school and received the manifestation of a screeching spirit, what some cultures call a banshee.

Peters had heard about the abandoned one-room schoolhouse, left unoccupied for a number of years and, as such, had no electricity and sported an outhouse. Interestingly, however, she said all of the building's windows were intact, something usually unheard of with forgotten buildings. It wasn't an easy trip for Peters to make, since she had previously injured her leg and was using crutches.

Peters tried searching for the schoolhouse again, sometime later, but said she couldn't find it. It's not an easy place to locate, she said, but noted it sits somewhere on a highway south of Aberdeen.

When they arrived at the school, they parked as close as they could so Peters didn't have to walk far with her injured leg. They entered the building, smelling the stale scent of the past, and started looking around. "After being there, I don't know, probably about ten minutes, there was suddenly a loud screeching sound," she recalled. She had her phone out to record the experience. "Thank goodness I got [the recording] on my phone," she said—before her daughter accidentally knocked it out of her hands.

Instead of waiting around to see what else would happen—if more screams would emit from the building or something more frightening happened—Peters decided they had better leave. But before they did, Peters thought it would be good to try to communicate their intentions with the screeching entity. She is usually not frightened by her paranormal experiences, but this one left her unnerved. She spoke aloud to the unseen presence, "We're leaving. I'm really sorry. We did this. I'm really sorry. Don't kill us. Don't do anything to us. We're leaving and I appreciate you letting us know that we're not welcome here."

It took her another ten minutes to get out of the schoolhouse, but she finally made it to the car. Since the episode occurred, Peters has had time to better analyze what it might have been that drove them from the abandoned building. "I have a few friends in other countries, in Scotland and Ireland, where they believe in banshees," she said. She sent her friends the recording and they responded, saying it sounded an awful lot like their banshees—which, according to Irish folktales, is a female spirit who, with her shrieking and wailing sounds, warns of impending death.

"That's just how they communicate," Peters said.

THE LITTLE LOST GHOST CHILD

ST. JAMES CHURCH AND CEMETERY, NEAR ENEMY SWIM LAKE

"Mommy, I'm right here," the young child's voice sounded.

But there was no child nearby to make the sound, no phantom voice echoing through the breezy afternoon. This phrase was heard only afterward when Peggy Peters played back the recording she had captured while investigating St. James Cemetery near Enemy Swim Lake on the Lake Traverse Indian Reservation in South Dakota's northeast region.

She had gone there—to this place with which she is personally connected because family is buried there—to test new, recently purchased equipment. It was broad daylight, and she could easily see the headstones dotting the graveyard. Like most cemeteries, some of the headstones lay flat and others are raised markers.

The cemetery has been there a long time, located in an isolated spot, she said. But it is meaningful to tribal members.

It was during this afternoon visit that she began to record video. In a clip she sent to me in July 2022, the video plays for several seconds, the wind whips the brush and trees. And then, startlingly, a child's voice is heard: "Mommy, I'm right here."

In another video clip she sent me from the same day, the camera pans the cemetery, recording the wind rustle the tree leaves, flowers and other emblems basking at the headstones, expressing movement in the wind. And, in the distance, at one of the markers, it captures what appears to be a woman in red sitting down. Then, the woman moves, bending forward. But again, according to Peters's natural eyes, no person was there that day dressed in red, sitting at the headstone.

These episodes—a child's voice, an adult woman's visage—were only detected by video recordings. Accordingly, the spirits at St. James haunt even in the light of day. Peters said there is nothing unusual about hauntings during the day. Paranormal activity happens all day long, and the sun doesn't have to set before things start to go bump in the night. They happen during the daytime, too.

And why wouldn't they? The energies that make up life are active throughout the day, not only when darkness falls. Perhaps they are more active during light hours, in fact, but us mortals are busier during the day and thus do not recognize such activity. It is only when the night falls and things quiet down that our senses pick up. According to Peters's recordings, spirits apparently roam their graveyards even in the broad light of day.

Also, Peters said, often when a spirit is seen, it is not as a mist or some transparent entity but as a real person—hard-pressed for a mortal to mark the difference—until the phantom dissolves into thin air as if it never existed. This belief is something Peters holds close to the vest, but it seems to be a belief among others as well. In speaking with various sources for this book, other paranormal investigators say much the same thing—that spirits often manifest themselves as real people, not ephemeral visages that rustle in the breeze like tree leaves.

"They appear as who they were in real life," she explained to me. "I've never known anyone to know someone to appear for longer than just a moment, so I'm not sure if they can maintain that for very long, if they actually have to have energy to maintain a more solid form. But I do know that from experience and from stories and teachings that they can have that solid form to them." Knowing this, she says: "That's why we are told to try and be nice when someone walks by us, when somebody is talking to us; we try to be polite and open-minded with them and not be rude or mean. People can have negative experiences in life, and even when they're dead can have negative experiences, and so we try to treat everybody decently."

MYTHICAL FIGURES, RED WATER, AND THE TRAIL OF SPIRITS

SICA HOLLOW STATE PARK, SISSETON

The Dakota Sioux stayed clear of the site, as much as possible, believing it to be a bad place better left alone. It was here, in what today is known as Sica Hollow State Park, where they believed mythical figures battled. The result of their conflict being spilt blood—actually red-tinted water likely caused by minerals—that the Sioux believed bubbled from nearby springs.

Strange stories about Sica Hollow (pronounced SHE-cha), including tales about the Trail of Spirits, have been passed down over the years. New stories, however, are being added from contemporary visitors who claim to have experienced things at the park that have left them dumbfounded, if not a little unnerved. Strange noises, such as moans and groans, dark figures in the woods, phantom war cries and drum beats, and campfires that mysteriously disappear are some of the legends told about this sacred site.

Peggy Peters, with South Dakota Paranormal Investigations, said the place is indeed sacred to her Sisseton tribe, though she couldn't explain exactly why. She only noted it has been passed down for decades as being a sacred place. Stories say that the hollow was an annual gathering place for the Dakota, but it also has a creation and vengeance story associated with it. It is believed that here is where mythical figures had once fought.

Peters said in a Facebook post on August 25, 2021, that she and a group of women she was with at Sica Hollow heard strange noises that seemed to follow them, from both sides of the road, for a period of time. At one point it sounded like a loud roar. "I don't know if they were following us to say goodbye, I don't really know what it was," she said in the post. "I don't want to believe it was anything malevolent."

The hollow is home to the Trail of Spirits, an eight-mile interpretive trail system that stretches through the woods. Designated a National Recreation Trail in 1971, it takes visitors through the scenic forest that, with its quietude, displays a haunting and beautiful scene. People who have walked the trail have reported its eerie silence, as if birds and wildlife—who live in abundance in South Dakota's forested hills—know better than to enter the nine-hundred-acre wooded area that comprises Sica Hollow.

Another story that continues today has its roots in the 1970s, when a group of campers entered Sica Hollow never to be seen again. Some people believed the backpackers were abducted by a hairy beast, perhaps a Bigfoot, that lived in the hollow. Others claimed to actually have seen a hairy manlike creature stalk the woods, thus fueling the legend.

When a team of searchers went looking for the missing hikers, they later admitted they also were searching for Bigfoot. Their efforts were to no avail; they never found the hikers nor any Sasquatch. But the legend persists, as does the question: What happened to the missing hikers?

Other people who have visited Sica Hollow say they have heard the sounds of drum beats in the distance, echoing through the woods, and have seen campfires through the trees. When hikers approach one of these campfires, they are nowhere to be found. They just disappear.

The scare scale of Sica Hollow, located about fifteen miles northwest of Sisseton off state Highway 10, varies from person to person, depending on their beliefs. Some believe the legends, others do not. For each of the stories, besides the supernatural answers, there are natural, more reasonable explanations; but for those who do believe in its haunted mysteries this site ranks a firm 10 out of 10.

Visit, if you dare!

RECOMMENDED READING

BOOKS

Barnes, Jeff. *The Great Plains Guide to Custer: 85 Forts, Fights & Other Sites.* Mechanicsburg, PA: Stackpole Books, 2012.

Barth, Aaron L. *Images of America: Fort Abraham Lincoln.* Charleston, SC: Arcadia Publishing, 2018.

Hedren, Paul L. *Traveler's Guide to the Great Sioux War: The Battlefields, Forts, and Related Sites of America's Greatest Indian War.* Helana, MT: Montana Historical Society, 1996.

Jackson, William. *The Best of Dakota Mysteries and Oddities.* Dickinson, ND: Valley Star Books, 2003.

Jacobs, Mike, ed. *Come Hell and High Water.* Grand Forks, ND: Grand Forks Herald, 1997.

Larson, Troy, and Terry Hinnenkamp. *Ghosts of North Dakota: North Dakota's Ghost Towns and Abandoned Places.* Los Angeles, CA: Sonic Tremor Media LLC, 2014.

Leppart, Gary. *Images of America: Medora and Theodore Roosevelt National Park.* Charleston, SC: Arcadia Publishing, 2007.

Orser, Lori L. *Spooky Creepy North Dakota.* Charleston, SC: Schiffer Publishing, Ltd., 2010.

Pechan, Bev, and Bill Groethe. *Images of America: Deadwood 1876–1976.* Charleston, SC: Arcadia Publishing, 2005.

Schell, Herbert S. *History of South Dakota.* Fourth edition, revised. Pierre, SD: South Dakota State Historical Society Press, 2004.

ONLINE

"10 Ghost Stories and Scary Tales that Prove South Dakota Is the Creepiest State." EverythingSouthDakota.com, August 12, 2018. https://www.everythingsouth dakota.com/10-ghost-stories-and-scary-tales-that-prove-south-dakota-is -the-creepiest-state/, accessed August 20, 2022.

"1941 United States Minimum Wage in Today's Dollars." *Dollar Times*. https://www.dollartimes.com/inflation/items/1941-united-states-minimum-wage, accessed July 2, 2022.

Bennett, Brianna. "Unfinished Business: North Dakota. 'She's Unhappy Here, and She Wants to Leave.'" *Medium*, April 23, 2021. https://medium.com/friday-night-crimes/unfinished-business-north-dakota-67a4491fc54, accessed July 8, 2021.

"Bigfoot saga continues in Ellendale, N.D." *Grand Forks Herald*, January 31, 2017. https://www.grandforksherald.com/newsmd/bigfoot-saga-continues-in-ellendale-n-d, accessed July 2, 2022.

"Bismarck." Britannica. https://www.britannica.com/place/Bismarck-North-Dakota, accessed July 2, 2022.

Briggs, Tracy. "Fargo's Most Famous UFO Sighting was in the Skies above a 1948 Bison-Augustana Football Game." *West Central Tribune*, December 20, 2020. https://www.wctrib.com/community/fargos-most-famous-ufo-sighting-was-in-the-skies-above-a-1948-bison-augustana-football-game.

"Carving History." National Park Service: Mount Rushmore National Park. https://www.nps.gov/moru/learn/historyculture/carving-history.htm, accessed July 2, 2022.

"Custer House." *Bismarck Tribune*, July 22, 2014. https://bismarcktribune.com/custer-house/article_19572b50-11e0-11e4-8a8e-001a4bcf887a.html, accessed July 1, 2022.

"Exploring Black Hill's Hidden Ghost Towns: Pactola," *Black Hills Visitor Magazine*, January 9, 2018. https://blackhillsvisitor.com/learn/pactola/#:~:text=The%20Pactola%20Dam%20was%20constructed,boating%2C%20swimming%2C%20and%20hiking, accessed July 8, 2022.

Gomez, Nathalie. "Little Chicago Pub District in downtown Minot." KXNet, June 13, 2018. https://www.kxnet.com/news/little-chicago-pub-district-in-downtown-minot/, accessed July 16, 2022.

Greenfield, Rebecca. "Our First Public Parks: The Forgotten History of Cemeteries." *The Atlantic*, March 16, 2011. https://www.theatlantic.com/national/archive/2011/03/our-first-public-parks-the-forgotten-history-of-cemeteries/71818/, accessed June 17, 2022.

"Gutzon Borglum: Mares of Diomedes, 1904." RISD Museum, https://risdmuseum.org/art-design/collection/mares-diomedes-29086, accessed July 2, 2022.

"Harvey Man Sent to Prison After Confessing Crime." *Bismarck Tribune*, October 6, 1931. https://www.newspapers.com/clip/4637176/front-page-sophia-eberlein -bentz/, accessed July 1, 2022.

"Harvey, N.D., Library Haunted? Library Workers Wonder." *Grand Forks Herald*, October 30, 2009. https://www.grandforksherald.com/newsmd/harvey-n-d -library-haunted-library-workers-wonder, accessed July 1, 2022.

"Haunted Outdoors of South Dakota." Travel South Dakota—South Dakota Department of Tourism. https://www.travelsouthdakota.com/trip-ideas/ haunted-outdoors-south-dakota, accessed August 16, 2022.

History, City of Minot, North Dakota. https://www.minotnd.org/338/History, accessed July 16, 2022.

"History of the Real Deadwood, South Dakota." https://www.deadwood.com/ history/.

Homestake Opera House. https://www.homestakeoperahouse.org/history.html.

Housholder, Grace. "Mount Rushmore was completed in 1941." KPC News, September 20, 2020. https://www.kpcnews.com/columnists/article_557bd15e -f384-53d7-ad5d-cc488c10dd8a.html, accessed August 19, 2022.

Howell, Jase. "Old Armory to Receive Renovation." *Williston Herald*, April 9, 2012. https://www.willistonherald.com/news/old-armory-to-receive-renovation/arti cle_6a6dba36-8268-11e1-b93f-001a4bcf887a.html, accessed July 8, 2022.

"James Comyon Sherman." Find a Grave. https://www.findagrave.com/memo-rial/31372191/james-comyon-sherman.

Lewis and Clark Trail. South Dakota Department of Tourism. https://www.travel southdakota.com/trip-ideas/article/lewis-clark-trail, accessed June 16, 2022.

"Lillian and Coleman Taube Museum of Art (Union National Bank and Annex)." Society of Architectural Historians. https://sah-archipedia.org/buildings/ND -01-WD5, accessed July 16, 2022.

"Mandan." Britannica. https://www.britannica.com/place/Mandan-North-Dakota, accessed July 2, 2022.

"Marquis de Mores." National Park Service: Theodore Roosevelt National Park. https://www.nps.gov/thro/learn/historyculture/marquis-de-mores.htm, accessed July 1, 2022.

Mid-Western Ghosts and Hauntings. http://midwesternghostsandhauntings.blog spot.com/2012/09/old-luger-hotel-and-legend-of-black.html, accessed June 29, 2022.

Moran, Berton. *Local Legends*. https://www.youtube.com/c/locallegendsberton moran, accessed June 25, 2022.

Mount Moriah Cemetery. City of Deadwood, South Dakota. https://www.cityof deadwood.com/community/page/mount-moriah-cemetery, accessed August 19, 2022.

Mount Rushmore: Carving History. National Park Service. https://www.nps.gov/ moru/learn/historyculture/carving-history.htm, accessed July 2, 2022.

Mount Rushmore: Hall of Records. National Park Service. https://www.nps.gov/ moru/learn/historyculture/hall-of-records.htm, accessed August 19, 2022.

Mount Rushmore: Memorial Lighting History. National Park Service. https://www .nps.gov/moru/learn/historyculture/memorial-lighting-history.htm, accessed August 19, 2022.

Mount Rushmore: Why These Four Presidents. National Park Service. https:// www.nps.gov/moru/learn/historyculture/why-these-four-presidents.htm, accessed July 2, 2022.

"Mrs. Sophia Bentz Burned to Death as Crash Pinions Her in Auto." *Bismarck Tribune*, October 2, 1931.

Mussulman, Joseph A. "Spirit Mound: An Elevation of Devilish Spirits." Discover Lewis and Clark Heritage Foundation. http://lewis-clark.org/the-trail/ nebraska-south-dakota/spirit-mound/, accessed June 16, 2022.

"North Dakota Records Several New Bigfoot Sightings: North Dakota Official Marks 'Bigfoot' on Map." Aberdeen American News, March 4, 2004, as quoted on BigfootEncounter.org. http://www.bigfootencounters.com/sbs/new town.htm, accessed July 2, 2022.

"Old Luger Hotel and The Legend of Black Tongue Hill—Fort Yates, North Dakota." Mid-Western Ghosts and Hauntings, September 2, 2012. http://midwestern ghostsandhauntings.blogspot.com/2012/09/old-luger-hotel-and-legend-of -black.html.

Olsen, W. Scott. "Ghosts at the Door: F-M's Oldest Gravesites Inspire Us to Celebrate Life, Even if Sometimes Scary." InForum, October 30, 2017. https://www .inforum.com/newsmd/ghosts-at-the-door-f-ms-oldest-gravesites-inspire-us -to-celebrate-life-even-if-sometimes-scary, accessed June 17, 2022.

"Pactola Reservoir: South Dakota's Version of Atlantis." South Dakota Department of Tourism. https://www.travelsouthdakota.com/trip-ideas/story/pactola -reservoir-south-dakotas-version-atlantis, accessed July 2, 2022.

"Paranormal Warm Spots: Ghost Hunting and Heat." Real Paranormal Experiences, Paranormal Warm Spots: Ghost Hunting and Heat—Real Paranormal Experiences. https://realparanormalexperiences.com/paranormal-warm-spots-ghost-hunting-and-heat/, accessed June 24, 2022.

Richardson, Jeanne. "The Creek That Thinks It's a River." *South Dakota Magazine*, January 9, 2018. https://www.southdakotamagazine.com/the-creek-that-thinks-its-a-river, accessed June 14, 2022.

Rodriguez, G. P. "UFO Hunter Spots '100,000-year-old alien face' that Looks like Mount Rushmore Carved onto Mars Mountainside." *The Sun*, September 22, 2021. https://www.the-sun.com/news/3714609/ufo-hunter-spots-alien-face-mount-rushmore-mars/.

Roth, Jenny. "Fall Haunts." *Aberdeen Magazine*, September/October 2018. https://aberdeenmag.com/2018/11/fall-haunts/.

Saad, Lydia. "Do Americans Believe in UFOs?" Gallup, July 2021; updated August 20, 2021. https://news.gallup.com/poll/350096/americans-believe-ufos.aspx.

Sica Hollow State Park (SD)—A Spooky and Beautiful Place. Legends of America. https://www.legendsofamerica.com/sd-sicahollowpark/.

"Sophia Schmidt Eberlein." Find a Grave. https://www.findagrave.com/memorial/176609079/sophia-eberlein, accessed July 1, 2022.

South Dakota State Historical Society. "Nearly 150 Years of Recorded UFO Sightings Across South Dakota." *The Capital Journal*, September 4, 2021. https://www.capjournal.com/community/nearly-150-years-of-recorded-ufo-sightings-across-south-dakota/article_e2321cb4-0cca-11ec-a9bd-9fb4adf435f1.html, accessed August 20, 2022.

"Spirit Mound Historic Prairie." South Dakota Game, Fish, and Parks Department. https://gfp.sd.gov/parks/detail/spirit-mound-historic-prairie/, accessed June 16, 2022.

Taube Museum of Art. https://taubemuseum.org/index.html, accessed July 16, 2022.

"The Haunted Indoors of Eastern South Dakota." South Dakota Department of Tourism. https://www.travelsouthdakota.com/trip-ideas/haunted-indoors-eastern-south-dakota, accessed July 8, 2022.

"The Keystone Cemetery is One of the South Dakota's Spookiest Cemeteries." https://www.onlyinyourstate.com/south-dakota/haunted-cemetery-sd/, accessed August 20, 2022.

"The Ghosts of Trollwood." High Plains Reader, January 18, 2017. https://hpr1.com/index.php/feature/culture/the-ghosts-of-trollwood/.

The Mars Rovers. NASA Science. https://spaceplace.nasa.gov/mars-rovers/en/.

"This Day in History: May 27—British navy sinks the German battleship Bismarck." History.com. https://www.history.com/this-day-in-history/bismarck-sunk-by-royal-navy, accessed July 6, 2022.

Tonsfeldt, Ali. "Ghosts of Fort Sisseton." South Dakota Game, Fish, and Parks. https://gfp.sd.gov/pages/ghosts-fort-sisseton/, accessed June 14, 2022.

Total Population for North Dakota Cities: 1920 to 2000. North Dakota State University. https://www.ndsu.edu/sdc/publications/census/NDcities1920to2000.pdf, accessed June 24, 2022.

Waring, Scott C. "Former UN Worker 'Finds Dead Alien and Mount Rushmore-Style Carvings' in NASA Mars Photos." *UFO Sightings Daily*: News About Us.

Walk with the Dead. Fargo's Riverside Cemetery. https://pocketsights.com/tours/place/Welcome-to-Riverside-Cemetery-6217:845.

"Welcome to LaFramboise Island." LewisAndClarkTrail.com, http://lewisandclark-trail.com/section2/sdcities/pierre/island.htm, accessed June 30, 2022.

"Why These Four Presidents?" National Park Service: Mount Rushmore National Park. https://www.nps.gov/moru/learn/historyculture/why-these-four-presidents.htm, accessed July 2, 2022.

Wiley, Payton. "Armory getting a new lease on life," October 19, 2012. https://www.willistonherald.com/news/armory-getting-a-new-lease-on-life/article_cebb371c-19fc-11e2-972b-001a4bcf887a.html?msclkid=2cee47e5c3dc11e-cbf4c81f6fe5b021d, accessed July 8, 2012.

Zander, Cecilyn N. "Libbie Custer's Literary Love Affair with Her Late Husband." HistoryNet, January 14, 2020. https://www.historynet.com/libbie-custers-literary-love-affair-with-her-late-husband/, accessed June 17, 2022.

ACKNOWLEDGMENTS

A number of people—business owners, park officials, museum curators and directors, local historians, and paranormal investigators—helped me with this book, and I wish to acknowledge them here. Life is busy, often hectic, and I appreciate and thank each of them for taking the time to visit with me, some by phone, others virtually, and some in person. They include the following:

In North Dakota, Wendy Kimble and Stephanie Pinkey of Paranormal Investigators of North Dakota (PIND), based in Minot, were extremely helpful in sharing their paranormal experiences with me and leading me to other sources and information. Like all good paranormal investigators, they want to get to the bottom of alleged hauntings and help people navigate their experiences. Their enthusiasm is contagious, and I thank them both for sharing it with me. I consider both Wendy and Stephanie friends and look forward to learning about their future adventures as they continue to investigate North Dakota's historic haunts.

Jim Bridger, owner of the Little Missouri Saloon in Medora and an old hospital in Sentinel Butte, in the western reaches of the state, was kind and helpful as he related personal experiences and other stories about his haunted locations.

Bambi Mansfield with the Billings County Courthouse Museum, also in Medora, shared the strange goings-on at the old facility. Deana Novak, president of the James Memorial Arts Center in Williston, North Dakota, gave me much information about history and hauntings at the arts center; and Chuck Wilder, a local historian and bookshop owner also in Williston, shared important information about the Old Armory. I also thank Diane Hagen, of the Old Armory, who led me to Wilder. Eric Hansen, owner of Urban Winery in Minot, and Rachel Alfaro, executive director of the Taube Museum of Art, also in downtown Minot, both shared fascinating stories about their respective sites.

Carolyn Boutain, enterprise director for the Fargo Park District, was extremely helpful—and enthusiastic—about sharing the history and background of Trollwood Park. She also put me in contact with other sources, including Vicki Chepulis, co-founder of the Trollwood Performing Arts School, who was also very kind.

Alexander Blue Weber, president and CEO of the Downtown Development Association in Grand Forks, North Dakota, who also hosts a historic walking tour, shared information—including his tour notes and map—about downtown sites. I enjoyed taking the tour with my wife and learning up close and personal about history and possible haunts of downtown Grand Forks.

Caedmon Marx, founder of Haunted Plains Paranormal Society and one of the youngest demonologists in the world, shared many personal experiences with me, some about historic sites, others about very personal encounters, and I appreciate his openness in doing so.

In South Dakota, Carolyn Johnson, museum interpreter at the Sioux Falls Heritage Museums, provided history and other information about the Pettigrew House and Museum and the Old Courthouse Museum in Sioux Falls, two of the city's stately, historic sites.

Peggy Peters, of Sisseton, founder of South Dakota Paranormal Investigations, was helpful in the early stages of this book, especially pointing me in the direction of another source, Andrea Steele of Sturgis, who lives in a very real haunted house. Later, as this book neared completion, Peggy shared videos and additional information with me. I thank them both for their insights and stories.

Kim Ferrel Keehn, a most excellent tour guide and founder of Haunted History Walking Ghost Tours in Deadwood, shared much information about her tour and the interesting, historic town that is Deadwood. Her passion for history—and the ghost stories it sparks—is contagious. Likewise, Louie Lalonde, general manager of Saloon No. 10, also in Deadwood, shared insight about her place of business.

Kevin Kuchenbecker, historic preservation officer with the Deadwood Historic Preservation Office, who also serves as sexton of Deadwood's historic cemeteries, provided information about Deadwood's most popular cemetery, Mount Moriah, and other historic tidbits.

Thomas Golden, executive director of the Homestake Opera House, in Lead, related stories, history, and his views of the paranormal.

Berton Moran, of Mitchell, who produces videos on YouTube called *Local Legends*, shared personal stories and perspectives about the paranormal, and I thank him for doing so and giving me deeper insight. Check out his videos on YouTube, they deserve a following.

Ali Tonsfeldt, manager of Fort Sisseton State Park, was enthusiastic about the stories of this historic site and shared a number of stories and historical tidbits. Her enthusiasm also is contagious.

Thank you, my sources and friends. I appreciate each of you for sharing your time, perspective, and stories with me. I hope I have done justice to the stories you shared with me. If by chance I got anything wrong, or have forgotten to mention anyone here, it was by human error and not deliberate intention.

Please, whenever you're in their neck of the woods, stop by to visit the historic sites. They all are worthy of recognition not just in a book, but by a personal visit. I tried to visit as many places as I could, but personal work constraints and having such a large coverage area prevented me from making all of the trips I wanted. But each of the sites are on my list, and I hope to one day visit those I missed.

I also thank Greta Schmitz, my editor at Globe Pequot, who took an interest in this book and who has been kind and pleasant to work with. As the book took shape, and the art was created, her enthusiasm grew. "I love it!" she said when she shared the cover with me. I do, too, and I thank the design team for its creepy creation. Schmitz and her team have done an exceptional job at streamlining and producing this book, designing the cover and inside art, and marketing this book. I hope the writing and reporting between its covers is worthy of the book's appearance. Many thanks to Jacqueline Plante, who edited the book and thereby made it better than it was before she put her sharp eyes upon it. I also am extremely thankful to Dominique McIndoe, assistant production editor, who was kind in many ways and, during the final stretch of production, allowed me extra days to complete editing when my schedule was already burdensome and hectic. I cannot say enough good things about my friends at Rowman & Littlefield Publishing Group, the parent company of Globe Pequot. You all are fantastic!

I appreciate family and friends who have encouraged my writing projects, which was especially needed during an extremely busy and stressful part of the year as I worked on the manuscript, wondering if I'd ever get it completed due to family matters and a busy work schedule. Sadly, my mom-in-law, Linda Snyder, who has always been excited and supportive of my writing projects, passed away during this project. We miss her, of course, and I am sad she is not here to read this book. I am sure it is one she would have liked. I also wish my own mom could have read this book, but, due to health problems, that has not been possible. Still, she was always encouraging with a mother's gentle love.

My wife, Heidi, was most encouraging, inspiring, and helpful—as always— and I cannot thank her enough for pushing me on those days when I felt, with all of life's stresses, that I had no more to give. She did this even as she also felt many of those same stresses. I thank her for reviewing the manuscript, offering suggestions, and helping with the bibliography. I also appreciate our son, Brayden, and daughter-in-law, Ashlyn, who, even though separated by many miles at the time of this project, asked about it and encouraged me. Eloise, who made me a proud grandfather, always put a smile on my face. She is my buddy!

My close friend, Craig Nytch, often asked how the book was progressing. He has always been enthusiastic and encouraging about my work, both as an author and a journalist. At a time when I worked alone a lot, he'd often call or text to share in good conversation and bring a smile to my face.

Good friend and fellow journalist Benito Baeza was also happy when he found I had written another book. I appreciate his excitement and listening ear. My friends' support means more to me than words can say.

I'd also like to acknowledge Korrie Wenzel, publisher of the *Grand Forks Herald* and *Prairie Business* magazine, who gave me the opportunity to live and work in North Dakota as a journalist covering business topics in three of what have become my favorite states—the Dakotas and Minnesota. I learned much from him, whether he knows it or not, by working with him up close and personal and by observing from afar. The lessons I gleaned have been about journalism and, more importantly, about life.

And I thank my colleagues while at *Prairie Business*—Nichole Ertman, Staci Lord, and Marsha Johnson—who helped make me feel a part of an important team, of which they truly are, while I was in North Dakota. I miss working with you all!

For all who have helped, lending their time, expertise, stories, and encouragement, thank you. I must say, however, that all of the conclusions and any errors of fact are my own doing and not theirs. This book is a private endeavor, and though I have tried to be historically correct and true to the stories and experiences shared with me, I apologize in advance for any oversight or mistakes in the telling of these tales of history and hauntings.

I also thank those authors and journalists who have contributed much to the historical and paranormal record that is the Dakotas. I respectfully acknowledge the state departments of tourism and their historic sites and the people who manage them, making sure these significant places are around for future generations. And I thank the businesses and organizations who opened their doors to me.

Finally, I want to thank you, the reader, for your interest, whatever it may be, in reading my book. There are millions of books to choose from, and you choosing to spend some time with mine means more to me than you'll ever know. I hope you like it.

ABOUT THE AUTHOR

Andy Weeks is an award-winning journalist and the author of several books on regional history and travel, some with a paranormal theme. His previous books in the Haunted States series include *Haunted Utah*, *Haunted Idaho*, and *Haunted Oregon*.

He enjoys traveling, being outdoors, and finding new adventures to write about. As a journalist, he has worked a number of beats, including business, education, and government, and produced everything from breaking news and investigative pieces to lifestyle and human-interest features.

He enjoys researching and writing a broad array of subjects, and finds telling the ghost stories of others, and those passed down in lore, an interesting way to help tell the history of an area. But people sometimes wonder, has this journalist, who chases facts for a living, had any of his own tales of the unexplained? In answer, he shares this story:

A door opens and footsteps pad across the bedroom. A moment later, I hear the clink of hangers being moved in the closet. I call to my wife from under the bedsheets, my face buried in a pillow. When my wife doesn't answer, I call again. The hangers stop making their noise. My wife, an early riser, was getting ready for work—or so I assumed—as she did most mornings at this time before I had to get out of bed. But why wasn't she answering me? After all, the closet was just a few feet away from our bed. I remove the pillow from my face and call again. When she still doesn't answer I pull the covers off, sit up, and look to the closet. The door is open, but the light is off. Hmm, I wonder. I turn to look at the clock on my nightstand—and goose pimples crawl up my nervous skin.

My wife had already left for work for the day—had been gone for a while, in fact, according to the red digital numbers that glare at me from a clock that sat atop my nightstand. Which left me with the question: Who, or what, had just entered our bedroom, walked across the room, and moved hangers in the closet?

I'm a journalist, I tell myself, a person whose profession and life-style deals with the facts of life, not its myths and mysteries. But, in an effort to be honest with myself, I admit that I had experienced enough of life's mysteries to know that sometimes things really do go bump in the night—and sometimes during the daytime, too.

Weeks, who has spent most of his life and career in the West, lived in North Dakota during the writing of this book and hopes one day to return to the prairie-land. He is currently working on his next writing project.